MW00979024

One Dog's Life

Robert Collings and Susan Hart

from a story by Robert Collings

ISBN-10: 1468191454

ISBN-13: 978-1468191455

Susan Hart & Robert Collings

In memory of my mother,
Jean Ella Collings

CONTENTS

ABOUT THE AUTHORS

Robert Collings is a lawyer and screenwriter in Vancouver, B.C. Susan Hart is his former literary agent. Bob currently has several original screenplays on the market. He owns the rights to the screenplay version of One Dog's Life, which is a fully developed original script. Bob also has another dark psychological thriller novel out, in conjunction with Susan Hart – *The Sum of All Evil*. This was also taken from another of Bob's original screenplays, written under the working title of *Demon Tango*.

****

Susan Hart was born in England but has lived on the Central Coast of California for many years, along with her husband and two cats. Her erotic thrillers, The Mozart Killer, Acting Like Death, and The Bone Picker (The Foxworthy Files) are on Kindle and in print, and they are also the first trilogy of The Foxworthy Files. She also wrote The Sum of All Evil with Bob Collings.

Susan Hart & Robert Collings

Chapter 1
(The Contest)

Penny was a little pug dog. She was a funny looking dog, and a lot of people laughed at her and called her ugly. She was also very lonely. She lived by herself in an abandoned warehouse on the outskirts of a town called Happy Valley.

One summer night, Penny sat at her usual spot on the rooftop of the warehouse, looking out at the distant lights of the carnival at the Happy Valley County Fair. Her frog-eyes bulged out of their sockets, and her long, pink tongue hung down from her mouth. How sad she looked! Penny wished she had friends who would go with her to the fair. But she was all alone that night, and all alone in life. As she looked at the lights, the faint sound of carnival music floated towards her on the summer air, and Penny tried to cheer herself up by thinking about better times and happier places.

Penny didn't know this, but she would not have been very happy at the carnival. There was a contest going on, and it was not the sort of contest she would ever want to win.

****

My name is Dinky, and I am one ugly dog! Oh, that gal on the rooftop there, that's not me. That's Penny. You'll meet Penny. Some people might call her an ugly dog, too. But believe me, by comparison I make Penny look like Lassie! I heard this joke once. A guy goes to the beach, and he was so ugly that a cat tried to bury him in the sand. Well, I'm here to tell you that ugliness is no laughing matter, even for dogs.

People, I used to complain about everything! I hated my ugly mug. And I hated waking up in the morning, because I knew the day ahead was going to be another mud-slog through the same old misery. And I guess if you're an ugly dog who wallows in his misery, someone out there might take pity on you and teach you a lesson. That's what I got, anyway. A real good lesson. Have you heard the old saying that a journey of a thousand miles starts with but a single step? Well, the first step on my journey into wisdom was the night my owner put me into that stupid contest!

****

The Happy Valley County Fair was always the biggest event of the year in the Pacific Valley, and this year was no exception. People were flooding through the carnival midway, and the barkers at all the games and attractions were making a fortune. The whole fair was blazing with bright lights and buzzing with the sounds of people having fun.

2

Two groups of people were approaching each other on the busy midway. With each group was a dog on a leash. If you were to get down low on the ground from a dog's point of view, you would have seen the dogs brush lightly against each other. And if you listened real hard, you might have heard the following:

"Sorry, friend," said the first dog.

"Hey, no problem!" said the second dog, cheerfully.

But no one heard the dogs speak, because no one ever listened.

Near the carnival midway was a huge outdoor theatre. A big sign at the side of the stage read:

'THE HAPPY VALLEY UGLY MUTT GRAND CHAMPIONSHIPS'

There was a crowd seated on the grass in front of the stage. In the background, the lights of the Ferris Wheel rose up against the sky, twirling and flashing in the summer night. Harold Briggs, the Mayor of Happy Valley, walked out onto the stage from behind the curtain and approached the microphone. He was a large man with a big smile. There was scattered applause from the crowd.

"Hello!" said Mayor Briggs. "As Mayor of this fine city..."

Suddenly, there was a loud cry from a baby in the crowd. Mayor Briggs shouted back: "Okay, free day care! We will find the money!"

This made the crowd laugh.

"As mayor of Happy Valley" he continued, "I bring greetings from ugly dogs worldwide! And I have the very great honor – I know it's a very great honor because it says so on this card they gave me to read out – I have the honor to introduce to you this year's Chamber of Commerce Ugly Mutt finalists. Just their dogs – dogs only! And from what I saw backstage, I think you folks are in for a grand and glorious treat tonight!"

Backstage, young kids were clutching their barking dogs, mothers and fathers were rushing about, and there was lots of noise and confusion.

Twelve year old Daisy Daniels was holding a little dog, but she was keeping a pink doggie-bonnet low over the dog's head, so no one could see his face. The dog was also wearing pink doggie-shorts with tiny holes for each of his skinny little legs. He was trying to get away, and Daisy was doing her best to calm him down. She spoke in a high pitched, spoiled whine.

"Okay, okay, tut-tut-tut-tut!" Daisy said, as she patted the squirming dog on the head.

On stage in front of the curtain, Mayor Briggs now read the first names from a slip of paper in his hand: "So let's welcome our first contestant! Tina Knowlan and Little Prince!"

Tina Knowlan bounced onstage from behind the curtain, pulling her dog on a leash. The dog looked blankly out at the crowd as he was tugged along. He didn't like being onstage, but he made no real fuss about it either. Little Prince was an ugly dog all right, but no prize winner. The crowd laughed and clapped politely.

4

Mayor Briggs then read out the next names: "Carly Wendorff and Elmer!"

Young Carly Wendorff hit the stage with her dog Elmer.

Elmer certainly was not a pretty face, but he was no prize winner either. There was more laughter from the crowd and more scattered applause. Mayor Briggs squinted through his reading glasses as he read the next names.

"Danny Sawatzke and Killer!"

Another ugly dog, but there were still more to come.

"Lita Miller and Caleb!"

"Johnny Walker and Spanky!"

"Kinsey Murdoch and Snoops!"

They were all ugly dogs, but the crowd didn't seem too interested. A few people got up and left, and the others looked bored and restless. Mayor Briggs continued to announce the names.

"Kyle Murdoch and Elvis!"

Young Kyle came out onstage, tugging his beloved Elvis. Elvis wore a doggie-Elvis costume and the fur on his face was trimmed to look like two long sideburns. Elvis would not budge, so Kyle dragged him across the stage. Elvis looked out at the audience as he was pulled across the smooth floor, and he raised one of his eyebrows as if to say 'hello'. He was an ugly Elvis to be sure, but he was no prize winner either.

The audience was now clearly bored, and there were a couple of loud boos from the back of the crowd. Mayor Briggs looked at all the dogs that were now lined up at the far side of the stage. He held up his list of names and looked down at the last two names on the list.

"Well, isn't this a handsome line-up?" he asked the crowd.

"We have our final contestant tonight! Let's have a big Happy Valley welcome for Daisy Daniels and...Dinky!"

Daisy now walked proudly onstage, holding her dog Dinky. His pink bonnet was still pulled low over his face. Daisy reached the center of the stage and gave a big grin and a wave to the audience. Then she lifted the bonnet so Dinky's face could now be seen by everyone. She placed Dinky on the stage in front of her and took a step back. Dinky was now all alone with nowhere to hide.

Unlike their reaction to the other dogs, the crowd reacted to Dinky - with silence. They stared up at the little creature on the stage, transfixed. They had never seen a dog like Dinky before.

Poor Dinky was the ugliest mutt in the world!

A woman pointed to Dinky and started laughing. More laughter followed, and soon the entire crowd was roaring with delight. As the laughter got louder and louder, all poor Dinky could do was sit still and stare out at the crowd, hoping and praying that the laughter would stop and he could soon go home and be alone. But the crowd did not stop laughing.

As the laughter continued, Daisy came over to Dinky and reached down and rubbed his stomach, This caused Dinky to grimace and break out into a wide grin. It was not a smile at all, because Dinky would be the last dog in the world to smile at people who were laughing at his ugliness. It was just an expression that Dinky could not help making. But the crowd loved it and laughed even louder.

Mayor Briggs knew there was no use in having a vote. He had found his winner already. He placed a big blue ribbon over the pink cap and over Dinky's head, and it slumped down over his hairless shoulders. Dinky stared straight ahead, and the crowd continued to laugh.

"Dinky Daniels," Mayor Briggs smiled, "Greet your adoring fans!"

The crowd cheered and clapped wildly. Dinky could do nothing but look out at them, expressionless, and wait for the humiliation to be over.

****

Daisy Daniels and her parents left the midway early. Mary Daniels was having a big party to celebrate the Happy Valley County Fair, and the best of Happy Valley society had been invited. This was Mary's chance to make a big impression, and she was not going to let this opportunity slip away. She was determined to make her mark on Happy Valley society with a party that no one would ever forget.

Mary had no way of knowing that she would indeed have a party that no one would forget – but for all the wrong reasons.

As the family drove along in their car, Mary was lost in thought. Daisy's father Clyde kept watching her, but he said nothing. Daisy and Dinky were in the back seat. Dinky still had the blue ribbon draped over his little body, and he was trying hard to forget all about the prize he had just won.

Mary's mind was racing, and she had a worried expression.

"I can't remember," she said to herself, "Did I tell those kitchen people to line the glasses up on the long table beside the fountain?"

"A million and twenty-six times," Clyde said with a smile. "But then I lost count."

"That fountain is gross!" Daisy said.

"Renaissance art is what it is!" her mother snapped back. "You need to cure your taste for ugly pets and get a little culture in your life! Look at the time! People are going to start arriving the second we get home!"

Clyde thought about this for a moment. "Tell ya what," he smiled, "We cancel our stuffy party, I'll spring for Chinese Food at Fong's, and our little family can just slo-oo-ow down. What do you say?"

"I'll slow down, my dear," Mary responded. "But you just drive faster!"

Clyde looked at her and said nothing. Mary grinned at him. Clyde knew all about that determined look on his wife's face, and he was smart enough not to argue the point.

Daisy leaned over and planted a big kiss on the top of Dinky's head.

"Mayor Briggs is coming to our house," she whispered to Dinky. "Isn't that exciting? He gave you the blue ribbon! Everyone's coming over!"

Dinky was not interested in any party.

He was not interested in seeing anyone.

All he wanted to do was find a quiet place to hide where no one would be laughing at him. He tried to control his wandering right eye, but as Daisy smothered him with kisses his eye slowly floated to the side and stared out the window. His other eye kept looking straight ahead. He knew how funny he looked, but it wasn't his fault.

He didn't want to be an ugly dog. Why did God choose to make him that way? He had done nothing to deserve his ugly mug. It wasn't fair!

Daisy would not leave him alone. "Just between you and me," she chirped, "I think you are the prettiest little doggie in the whole dog-gone world!"

Daisy continued to smooch Dinky on the top of his pink bonnet. Patches of black dog hair shot out from the sides of the cap like weeds. Dinky cowered and moved his tongue from one side of his mouth to the other. He continued to stare in two directions at once, likely the only dog in the world that was capable of such a feat.

It was a distinction that brought him no happiness.

9

Chapter 2
(The Angel)

The party guests had not yet arrived, and Mary Daniels was busy supervising the kitchen staff that had been hired especially for the occasion. She inspected all the champagne glasses lined up on the counter.

"We'll do this one last time," Mary announced. "Two, four, six, eight..."

In the dining room, an impossibly long table had been decorated with food. Each little cake and sandwich was perfectly arranged in its own place, like pieces in a gigantic jigsaw puzzle. At the head of the table was an enormous two-tier crystal punch bowl that had been set up like a fountain, with matching crystal glasses and tiny lights that sparkled through all the limes and the lemons and the dark red liquid. It was a dazzling display.

Standing above the punch bowl was the ceramic figure of a cherub with rosy cheeks and a mischievous grin. The cherub was peeing a red stream of fruit punch into the fountain. The shining red liquid tumbled over the rim of the fountain into the main punch bowl. When the bowl was nearly full, a tiny pump would start automatically and send a stream of punch back up to the cherub to repeat the cycle.

Mary Daniels had covered every detail in her quest to reach the top of Happy Valley society.

Daisy walked by the punch bowl and looked at the grinning cherub, peeing cheerfully away in a never-ending stream of red fruit punch. Daisy scrunched up her nose and made a face.

"Oh, how gross!" Daisy exclaimed.

****

The guests started to arrive. Soon, the entire street was filled with cars. A steady stream of people made their way up the stone walkway to the front door of the house. Everyone was dressed in their finest clothing. The men wore tuxedos and the women were all decked out in shining, long ball gowns. Mary Daniels stood at the front door and greeted each guest with a huge smile. Her party was going to be the biggest social triumph in the history of Happy Valley! Mary became especially animated when Mayor Briggs and his wife appeared at the door.

"Mayor Briggs!" Mary beamed. "I'm delighted you could come!"

Mayor Briggs nodded to a huge woman beside him. She was dressed in a gaudy white gown that looked like a cross between a wedding dress and a circus tent. "You know my wife, Esther?"

"Of course!" Mary exclaimed. "We worked together on the decorating committee. Hello Mrs. Briggs!"

Esther Briggs did not respond. She looked past Mary and walked into the house. "Where's that ugly little dog?" she asked. "He reminded me of my first husband. Harold! What was that little man's name?"

"There's been so many of them," Mayor Briggs muttered, "I don't remember them all."

Everyone laughed, and the sound of the laughter started to filter upstairs.

Dinky was upstairs, alone in his doggie-bed in Daisy's bedroom. He was still wearing his pink bonnet and shorts, and he still had the blue ribbon draped around his neck. He could hear the laughter from the party. And as hard as he tried, he could not forget all the cruel laughter from the contest at the fair. For him, it was never going to end. He laid his head down on the little bed and closed his eyes. A single tear spilled out of his wandering right eye and rolled down his face onto the blue ribbon.

It would never end, all the laughter. Ever.

Dinky lay with his eyes closed, alone and crying, when he was suddenly aware of a bright light in the room. He opened his eyes. Hovering in front of him were two tiny winged creatures, one with the face of a dog and the other with the face of a cat. But these peculiar little creatures were dressed just like the party guests downstairs, as if they were going to their own grand society ball.

The little angel-creatures stared at Dinky. They looked sad, as if Dinky's own sadness had somehow made both of them unhappy.

They moved a little closer, still suspended in mid-air, and they started to make tiny, low-pitched squeaking sounds. They were sounds of sympathy that told Dinky that someone might understand his misery after all.

Then, the light in the room got even brighter and Dinky was blinded. As he blinked his eyes and tried to adjust to the light, he heard a voice just behind the little angel creatures that buzzed in front of him.

"Blink your eyes, Dinky," the voice said. "And, please don't be afraid."

Dinky blinked, once, twice, and then his eyes fell on the most beautiful lady he had ever seen. She was an angel too, surrounded by radiant white light. She had golden hair and huge golden wings that almost filled the room. She wore a flowing white gown that moved gently as she spoke, as if it was rippled by a breeze from a place far, far away.

"There!" said the angel. "I'm not so frightening, am I?"

Dinky was stunned, yet in the angel's presence he felt a sense of relaxation sweep over him at the same time. It was a curious sensation.

"Who are you?" Dinky asked.

"You don't know my name?" The angel smiled. "My name is Miranda, and I'm the guardian angel of all God's creatures. I watch over them and protect them. Even you, Dinky."

Dinky did not believe her. He slowly laid his head down on the bed.

"No one watches over me," he said, closing his eyes again.

****

Downstairs, the party was showing all the signs of becoming a big social success, and Mary Daniels was beaming as she walked through the crowd. Everyone she had invited had showed up, and all the party guests seemed to be having a splendid time. Mary was paying a great deal of attention to the Mayor's Wife. In fact, she had not let Mrs. Briggs out of her sight since she had arrived with her husband.

"Now, my dear Mrs. Daniels," said Esther Briggs, sipping from the cup of tea that Mary had just poured for her, "I positively will not leave this house until you show us that – that dog – that *creature*!"

Some of the guests had gathered around Esther Briggs and they all laughed.

"Alvin!" said Esther Briggs, suddenly remembering the name. "That was the name of my first husband! That dog reminds me of my poor homely Alvin!"

Everyone laughed again.

In the kitchen nearby, the staff was looking at something unusual. The family parakeet was in his cage in the corner of the room, but it stood rigid on its perch with his head tilted in the direction of Daisy's room upstairs. The bird was staring intently and it did not move. It was like it had turned to stone.

"Look at this silly bird!" exclaimed one of the staff.

"Hey, look at the fish!" said another, pointing to a small fish tank on the kitchen counter.

There was only one fish in the tank, a little goldfish. It had gone to the edge of the tank and was pressing its face against the glass. It was not moving either, yet it did not sink to the bottom of the tank. It seemed like the fish was suspended in the water by magic. Just like the parakeet, the lone goldfish was also staring straight ahead in the direction of Daisy's room.

"Nutty place," muttered someone else, and the staff went back to work.

****

Upstairs, Dinky still lay on his doggie-bed with his eyes closed. The little angel creatures still floated in the air and made their tiny sounds. Miranda smiled and kneeled down beside Dinky.

"Do you know nothing but sorrow and regret over your situation in life, Dinky?" Miranda asked. "Do you not realize how lucky you really are to have a home and family?"

The angel creatures then fluttered into Miranda's arms and she held them close.

"You see Dinky, I know Heaven. Heaven is a place of much goodness. But that goodness depends upon what we do here, on earth. That's true for people, and it's also true for dogs just like you."

"I don't want to be a dog," Dinky said, his eyes still closed.

Miranda leaned closer to Dinky and spoke in a whisper.

"But there are people who don't want to be people," she said. "And there are cats in this world who want to be dolphins, and antelopes who would rather fly like eagles so they don't have to run from their enemies. Don't you understand? The goodness in Heaven does not spring from what we wish to be, it springs from what we are. And we can never change what we are."

"Then Heaven can not a place with me in it," Dinky said. "You should leave me alone. I'm sorry."

"But we are not here to leave you alone, Dinky," Miranda said. "Our business is with you. You might be surprised to learn that you have won something more than the blue ribbon tonight. I have another gift for you, Dinky. And my gift...is your last chance to be happy."

Curious now, Dinky lifted his head off the bed and stared at Miranda.

Miranda continued: "You will be made human for twenty-four hours. At the end of that time, you will be given one wish, and one wish only. If you are happy with your human form, then human you stay, and I will put the wealth of the world at your feet if you so wish. Or, you might want to use the wish to become a dog again..."

"Never!" Dinky interrupted.

Miranda smiled knowingly. "Twenty four hours, Dinky. And then only one chance to again become the creature God made you."

"One wish?" asked Dinky.

"Remember me, and use the time wisely my little friend," Miranda told him. "But, above all, remember the wish. The thing you so desperately want will not be as you think, and the one wish will not be easy. Good-bye!"

"Wait!" Dinky shouted. "When is all this going to happen?"

But there was no answer. In an instant, Miranda and the little creatures had disappeared and Dinky was alone again. The only sound was the tick-tick-ticking of the doggie-clock on the bedroom wall. It was 9:30 exactly.

In the kitchen, the parakeet now relaxed and swung on its perch, and the goldfish started to move slowly through the green plastic plants in the tank. But no one had noticed.

In the living room, Esther Briggs and a group of the party guests now had Daisy Daniels backed up against a wall. They were not going to be denied.

"I've waited long enough, child!" laughed Esther Briggs, holding up her camera. "You just run upstairs and fetch that little doggie! I simply have to have a picture, or no one on this earth will believe me!"

"Yes! Yes!" the other guests all agreed.

Daisy loved the attention. "Okay!" she said, and she raced upstairs to fetch the ugliest dog in the world so the party guests could take pictures and laugh at them with their friends.

When Daisy reached her bedroom, she flung the door open.

"Dinky!" Daisy shouted, brimming with excitement. "Oh, Dinky! You are the most famous dog in all of Happy Valley!"

But Dinky's doggie-bed was empty, and Dinky did not seem to be in the room. Puzzled, Daisy stepped further into the bedroom and looked around. She noticed something unusual on the floor beside Dinky's bed. On closer inspection, it was a single white feather. When Daisy reached out to pick it up, the feather rose up from the floor and started to gently spin around. Up, up, it went, spinning faster all the time, until it vanished through the ceiling.

Daisy was frightened now, and her eyes darted about the room.

"Dinky!" she called out. "Dinky, where are you?"

Then Daisy heard a noise behind her and she spun on her heels. She did not see Dinky, but now she was aware that someone, or something, was hiding behind the open bedroom door. Daisy paused, then took a short step forward.

"Dinky?"

Daisy took another step and stopped. Something was wrong.

"Who's there? Dinky, is that you?"

Suddenly, the door slammed shut and there against the wall stood Dinky the dog as an adult human. He was wearing a full-size pink bonnet and full-size frilly pink shorts held up by long pink suspenders. The blue ribbon, now adult-size, was still slung around his bare shoulders. Dinky's face was flushed red with excitement, brighter than his crazy pink outfit, and his eyes were as round as two full moons.

He ran up to Daisy, bouncing with joy.

"Daisy! Daisy! It's me, Dinky! The angel made me human! It's a miracle!"

Dinky gave Daisy a huge hug, and lifted her off the ground.

"It's a miracle! A miracle! A miracle!" Dinky shouted over and over, as he jumped up and down with Daisy in his arms. "I'm human forever!"

Daisy was unable to utter a single sound.

****

Downstairs, everyone was waiting for Daisy to return from the bedroom. All eyes were turned to the upstairs hallway and the closed bedroom door. Esther Briggs waved her camera in the air, waiting to get the first picture as soon as Daisy came out of the room with Dinky in her arms. Mary Daniels stood beside her, holding the pot of fresh tea, thrilled that her big party was becoming such a success.

"What an absolutely wonderful party, my dear," said Esther, as Mary filled her cup with more tea. "This is the most fun I've had since poor Alvin's funeral! It couldn't be more perfect!"

Then, a piercing scream came from the bedroom and the entire crowd fell silent. It was a silence that was quickly shattered by another scream, and then shattered again by the voice of Dinky himself as he ran out of the bedroom and hurried along the hall to the top of the stairs.

"The angel of all dogs made me human!" Dinky shouted. "This is a great moment of history! Get your cameras! Sound the bells! I am Dinky the dog and I am made human!"

Dinky stood at the top step and stared down at the party guests. They were stunned at first, and everyone just gawked at the stranger in the frilly pink shorts and doggie-bonnet. Then someone started to laugh, and more laughter soon followed. A few of the guests even started clapping.

"What's this?" Esther Briggs sniffed. "This some sort of vulgar stunt from the carnival?"

Mary Daniels said nothing. She just stared up at the intruder at the top of the stairs. Her lips parted slightly, and she did not even notice that she was spilling her teapot all over the freshly shampooed carpet.

Dinky did not understand the odd reception he was getting. Did the party guests not get it through their heads what he was trying to tell them?

"It's me! Dinky! Don't you all know who I am? "I'm...I'm..."

Dinky began to touch himself, his head, his upper body, his stomach. Then he reached lower still. Startled by his new body parts, he jumped up and slapped his hands against his thighs.

"*Human!*"

The party guests did not know what to do. If this was a joke, it was a strange joke and they were not sure how they were supposed to react. Everyone looked at Mary Daniels for some sort of sign, but all Mary did was stand with her mouth open, still staring at the crazy stranger in the pink doggie-shorts. It was like she did not quite know where she was.

Dinky slowly walked down the stairs, gesturing to the guests as he went. *Think, think!* Dinky said to himself. *Make a good impression!*

"I bring greetings from ugly dogs worldwide!" Dinky shouted. "Don't be alarmed, I know what some of you are thinking! Our friends from the animal kingdom are generally four-legged creatures called quadrupeds! They rarely dress themselves and they possess limited communication skills! So you say, how is it possible that a two-legged man-dog stands upright and speaks to us in our own language? I am living proof of the power and the divine grace of the guardian angel of all God's creatures! Through her infinite power of love a dog becomes...*flesh!*...and walks among you!"

Dinky reached the bottom step, and the guests stepped back .

"Hallelujah!" Dinky roared. "Rejoice and go forth all ye blessed people of Happy Valley! For this day I make all of you my disciples of doggie-joy!"

Dinky was not certain what to do once he reached the main floor. Instinctively, he reached out and shook the hand of the first person he met. This was Walter McKlosky, Happy Valley's eldest resident at age 104. Walter smiled politely as Dinky started to pump his arm up and down.

"Greetings, Walter!" Dinky smiled. "You're still alive, which baffles everybody!"

Dinky moved on, but Walter kept smiling and shaking an imaginary hand. Then, Dinky recognized another face near the stairs and he pushed his way through the crowd.

"Mrs. Matthews! It's Dinky! You know me! You were dog sitting and I chased your stupid cat and you tried to bash my brains out with the fire poker! I'm really, really sorry your cat got squashed by that garbage truck! Hey, maybe it's a dolphin now in its new life! You see, the angel told me all about that, she made me human, but only for a day...*Mommieeeeeee!*"

Dinky had spotted Mary Daniels. She was now standing in a puddle of hot tea. As she held the empty teapot upside down, the teabags slid out and plopped onto the rug. Mary didn't even notice. Her mouth was still open and her eyes were glazed over, as if she had just awoken from a bad dream. The crowd parted for Dinky as he ran up to her, waving his arms and hands in wild celebration.

"Mommy! Mommy! Isn't it wonderful? In my new human form, I don't even have the slightest inkling to chase my tail anymore! I now understand the logical impossibility of my own canine obsessions! It's me! This is what I used to do! Watch! You'll know it's me!"

Dinky now fell down on all fours and started to circle around Mary's legs, frantically biting and snapping at his imaginary doggie-tail.

"Look at me! Remember I used do this all the time? Where's my tail! Where's that old tail of mine? I'll bite it to smithereens! Lemme at it! *Gnah! Gnah! Gnah!*"

Roaring around in circles on his hands and knees, Dinky lost track of his direction and now found himself in total darkness. He had crawled under Esther Brigg's voluminous ballroom gown.

"Hey, it's real dark and scary in here!"

Dinky popped his head out from under the dress, and saw Esther Briggs' menacing figure towering over him. She was not amused.

"Get out from under me this instant!" Esther barked. "Have you no sense of etiquette or decorum, sir? If this has all been arranged as some sort of joke, I assure you, sir, I-am-not-laughing!"

Esther then shot an angry look at Mary Daniels.

"It seems that certain people around here think certain things are funny!"

Esther's hardened gaze landed on her husband who was standing at the other side of the room.

"Harold, let's go!"

Dinky rose to his feet and came face to face with Esther.

"It's you!" said Dinky. "I know you!"

"Harold!"

"You're the lady who pees real loud!"

"Well-I-never!" stammered Esther.

"Yes-you-did!" mocked Dinky, turning to the guests. "She farts in the corner, too!"

This little exchange was cut short by the sound of Daisy screaming from the stairs. In all the confusion, everyone had forgotten about her. She ran down the stairs and charged at Dinky and leaped onto his back. The two of them started to spin furiously round and round towards the long food table near the kitchen.

"You kidnapped Dinky!" Daisy screamed. "Bring him back, you criminal! Daddy! Daddy!"

Clyde Daniels stood rooted to the spot with the rest of the astonished guests, like a stranger in his own home. Daisy continued to scream and ride around on Dinky's back. Dinky tried to shake her off, but the more he tried, the more determined Daisy was to hang on.

"Help! Help me!" yelled Dinky. "Get this wretched, spoiled brat offa me!"

"Criminal! Criminal!" shouted Daisy. "Daddy, make a citizen's arrest! Mother!"

This seemed to bring Mary Daniels to her senses.

"Clyde!" she bellowed. "Do something!"

Clyde didn't move. As Daisy screamed, Esther Briggs decided to take charge. She ran over to Dinky and Daisy and took a firm grip on Dinky's pink suspenders.

"You leave this house this instant, you perverted human!" she commanded. "You are a desperately sick man!"

Esther Briggs pulled violently on Dinky's suspenders. Dinky now had Daisy riding around on his back and frantically pounding her fists on his head, and Esther Briggs twirling around in front of him, holding on to his suspenders with a fierce determination. Pressed together in this crazy dance, the three of them now spun around one last time towards the food table.

Esther stumbled backwards, the guests scattered away from the table, and the three of them – Daisy, Dinky, Esther – sailed full-tilt onto the long table. The table held for a few seconds, then came crashing down under their combined weight. Esther landed on the bottom, still clutching Dinky's pink suspenders. Dinky was squashed in the middle, gasping for breath. And Daisy ended up on top of the human pile, still screaming at the top of her lungs for her missing dog.

This was another type of sandwich, but not the kind that Mary Daniels ever had in mind.

Esther Briggs was stunned by the crash, and she lay motionless in the mess of squashed sandwiches and splattered desserts. She let out a low moan, but she didn't move. Her head had landed near the punch bowl, which had broken in two when the table collapsed. Remarkably, the ruddy-cheeked cherub had remained upright in all the destruction, and he continued to grin happily as he peed his last stream of red liquid directly into Esther's half-open mouth.

Mayor Briggs ran over and looked down at his wife. The punch was now spilling out of her mouth and running down both sides of her cheeks. Mayor Briggs looked at Clyde Daniels, who had hurried over to the collapsed table.

"Does this punch contain any alcohol?" Mayor Briggs asked.

"Yes, a little I think," responded Clyde, still stunned by what he had witnessed.

"It is no secret that Mrs. Briggs does enjoy her sherry from time to time," snorted Mayor Briggs. "And I am not criticizing the quality of the beverage. But this is quite unacceptable, sir!"

Some of the other guests tried to comfort Daisy, and Dinky was able to rise to his feet. He looked at Mary Daniels and slapped his rear end.

"See?" Dinky beamed, "No tail!"

Hysterical now, Mary turned to her husband one last time.

"Do something!" she bellowed.

But Clyde could do nothing. He stared at Dinky, who simply gave him a bewildered smile.

****

The party guests were all crowded around the front door when the police lead Dinky out of the house to the waiting police van. He was handcuffed, and still wore his pink bonnet and frilly pink shorts.

"This is all a big mistake!" he pleaded, as they led him away. "That's my family in that house!"

"You picked the wrong party, lover-boy," said one of the police officers.

"I'm a dog! I just look human!"

"Well, you got one up on my sister! She's a dog, and she looks like a dog!"

"You don't even have a sister!" laughed the other officer.

"No! You don't understand!" Dinky pleaded.

The police officer was in no mood to negotiate. When they reached the van, he opened the door and pointed to the back seat. In the very back of the van, behind a wire grate, Rex the police dog watched Dinky with a wary eye. Dinky looked at him and stared.

"That dog talks!" Dinky said. "Doesn't anyone around here ever listen?"

"Get in!"

The officer pushed Dinky into the back seat of the police van and slammed the door. Dinky Daniels was then taken away from his family for the very first time in his life.

Chapter 3
(Here Comes The Judge)

The Happy Valley Police station was quiet that night. But, that was nothing new. Happy Valley was pretty much a crime-free city. The Happy Valley police spent a lot of time polishing their vehicles and sweeping the station floor, but no one could remember the last time any of them had actually chased a real criminal.

The police brought Dinky into the station, still handcuffed. Rex followed obediently behind, ever the faithful police dog. Dinky was led down a narrow corridor to a small holding cell. When they reached the cell, one of the officers unlocked the handcuffs and they slipped off Dinky's wrists. The officer gently pushed Dinky into the cell, then he closed the door and it banged shut with a loud 'clang'! While the first policeman locked the door, the other officer glared at Dinky.

"You sure you don't want to tell us your real name?" he asked.

Dinky didn't respond. He slumped down on the little bed under the window and put his head in his hands. He wondered how he had ever got himself into such a mess. The two policemen waited for a few moments, then they walked back down the hall towards the main desk.

"He'll give his name to Judge Levitts, that's for sure!" one of them remarked.

Dinky looked around the little cell. The window above his bed had bars on it so no one could escape. It was the sort of window that was left open all summer, and Dinky could feel a slight breeze coming in from outside. As he reached for a blanket that was rolled up at the foot of the bed, he heard a voice outside from beneath the window.

"Hey, Mr. Dinky! I'm out here!"

Dinky got up on the bed and stood on his tiptoes and looked out the window. There in the empty parking lot below stood Penny, the homely pug dog who lived in the abandoned warehouse. There was a single street light nearby, and Dinky was able to get a glimpse of the tiny stranger. She was all black, but had a patch of snow-white fur on her forehead in the distinctive shape of a diamond.

"My name's Penny!" said the little dog, with a smile. "All of us stray dogs in the city, we know all about you! It's dangerous for us at night, so we drew straws to see who was gonna come and say hi. I lost, as usual. Hi!"

Before Dinky could respond, he heard one of the policemen calling to him from down the hall.

"Hey, fancy-pants, you got a visitor!"

"Watch out for the dog-prison!" warned Penny.

Penny then scampered across the parking lot and her little form quickly faded into the darkness. Dinky had just lowered himself on the bed when he saw Clyde Daniels appear at the cell bars.

"They told me at the desk that you won't give your name," Clyde said. He did not look upset. On the contrary, he seemed quite cheerful.

Clyde pulled a nearby chair towards the cell and sat down.

"Son, you are looking at a man who lives with two crying women, one parakeet, one goldfish, and no dog." Clyde smiled and shook his head. "That little mutt, he was the most pitiful creature you ever saw, lying there all alone in the dog pound. Everyone pointing at him and laughing. His mother died in the workhouse. Lord only knows who his father was. Nobody else would take him, except me."

Dinky did not want to hear about his past. "Your daughter wants a toy – buy her a Slinky next time," he said. "And you can stick an ugly face on it!"

"You ruined my wife's big society bash, you know," Clyde said. "Personally, I don't care. But maybe you should care a little."

"What time is it?" Dinky asked.

"Son, I don't care what your name is, and I don't care how you got into our house. Just give my Daisy her dog back and go live your life. Could you do that for us?"

"I don't know the time!" Dinky said. "I don't have anything! No clothes, nothing!"

"The time is about two minutes past midnight," Clyde said, looking at his wristwatch.

Dinky looked earnestly at Clyde. "Mr. Daniels, I may have been a little hasty in what I wished for. Maybe the angel was right. Your daughter will get her dog back at 9:30 tonight, I promise you."

This made no sense to Clyde, but Dinky sounded so sincere that he didn't argue. Of course, Clyde Daniels was not the sort of person to argue with anyone. He rose from his chair and smiled kindly at Dinky.

"Okay, then," said Clyde. "See you tonight, 9:30."

Clyde turned to walk away, and Dinky ran up and pressed his face between the cell bars.

"Mr. Daniels! Hey!"

Clyde stopped and looked back at him.

"That ugly dog. What was gonna happen to him?"

"If I didn't take him?" Clyde said. "He was going to be put to sleep, of course. The joke was, he had about thirty seconds left before I came along."

"Funny joke," said Dinky.

"9:30, son," said Clyde. "You promised!"

Clyde reached the far end of the hall, and Dinky shouted to him one more time.

"Don't let that wife of yours try to kick you up the social ladder! You are the man she married! You're better than the man she married!"

31

Clyde reached the main desk of the station and headed for the door.

"Everything okay sir?" asked the desk sergeant.

"Everything's fine," said Clyde. "Good-night."

****

The Happy Valley Courthouse had stood in the town center for as long as anyone could remember. It was a big, old, southern-style building with long columns lining the main entrance and a marble stairway leading up to the imposing front doors.

Dinky sat in Courtroom #1 waiting for his case to be called. The room was packed with lawyers and people who had every manner of legal problem. Some lawyers huddled with their worried clients, while others shouted at each other from the far corners of the room. The whole courtroom seemed to shake with the sound of a hundred different voices.

Dinky had been a human for less than a day. He could not have felt more out of place if he had been dropped on the moon.

The Daniels family sat in the front row of the gallery. Dinky caught Clyde's eye, and Clyde nodded. Mary Daniels refused to even glance at the man who had ruined her party, and she kept a hard stare straight ahead. And when Daisy looked at Dinky it was only so she could make an angry face and stick out her tongue. The justice system was coming straight at him, and he would have to take it alone.

The court clerk stood up and said in a loud voice: "All rise!"

In an instant, the busy room fell silent. One of the policemen guarding Dinky poked him in the ribs.

"Stand up!" he said in a harsh whisper.

Dinky rose to his feet just as Judge Levitts entered the room.

"Court is in session!" said the clerk. "The Honorable Joseph P. Levitts presiding!"

Judge Levitts was an ancient, red-faced man, with huge, black, bushy eyebrows and a scowl that had been passed down to him through a hundred generations. He reminded Dinky of an angry crow.

"Call the first case!" Judge Levitts snarled.

"The People versus Dinky!" the court clerk announced.

There was scattered laughter from the gallery, and Judge Levitts banged his gavel down hard on the huge oak bench. Dinky was not sure what to do, and the policeman pushed him forward.

"Go on!" the policeman said, giving him another push. "Just answer the judge's questions, and don't be a smart-ass."

Shell-shocked and exhausted, Dinky took a few steps towards the bench. He was not accustomed to his human legs, and he wobbled as he walked. The county prosecutor was standing at a table near the judge's bench, and as Dinky got closer the prosecutor held up a yellow sheet of paper.

"The People oppose bail, your Honor!" said the prosecutor, waving the sheet of paper with a dramatic flair. "This man is a threat to himself and everyone else in the community."

Judge Levitts looked through a stack of documents in front of him. "What sort of threat?" he muttered. "Who is this man?"

"He answers to only one name," said the prosecutor. "And, he insists he's a dog! And if that isn't enough, he drinks from the toilet! People like that are all in padded cells, Your Honor."

"You haven't seen our Supreme Court," muttered Judge Levitts, privately amused at his own wit.

There was more laugher at this remark, and Judge Levitts banged the gavel again.

"And you!" Judge Levitts snapped to Dinky, "Why do you approach the bench like a drunk? Didn't you sleep it off last night?"

Before Dinky could respond, the court clerk stood up and leaned over to Judge Levitts.

"Your Honor," the clerk whispered quietly, "Do you remember that Judicial Review Committee? You know, their comments about your attitude towards, ah, certain people who might be a little funny in the head? The *election* in two months?"

A light bulb now went off inside Judge Levitt's head, and be broke into a wide grin.

"You are a little unsteady on your feet, my friend!" he smiled to Dinky.

"I'm not used to walking with two human legs, my friend!" Dinky smiled back.

"What is your name, sir?"

"Dinky."

"Dinky. Okay, what's your last name?"

"My last name is my first name, sir."

"Not only is that philosophically impossible sir, it is also idiotic. You see, Mr. Dinky, everyone has two names. There is your surname, common to your family, and then there's your Christian name."

"I am a non-denominational dog, sir. I am neither Christian nor Jew."

"But I am of the Jewish faith, Mr. Dinky. And my last name is Levitts."

Judge Levitts now pointed to the name plate in front of him.

"You see?" he went on. "There it is. L-E-V-I-T-T-S! I also have a first name! I have two names! And, some of our brothers and sisters gathered in my courtroom today are of the Christian faith. They believe in a book called The New Testament. *They* have two names! Now I ask you once again sir, what is your last name?"

"The New Test...I never read that book," Dinky said.

"The Jews have never read it either, sir, but we hear it has a surprise ending!"

"Tell me!" Dinky said excitedly, "I ain't gonna spill the beans to no one, I promise!"

"We are getting off topic, sir!"

Judge Levitts was now sweating. He took a deep breath.

"I'll help you with your last name. What last name do you give on a job application?"

Dinky thought about this. "What's a job apple-caution?"

"A job-*application* sir! Have you never been employed?"

"Well, no."

"You have never held a job in your life? Is this what you are telling me?"

"Well, I don't need money."

"You steal your clothing, do you?"

"I don't need clothing, either."

"Yes, you do," snapped Judge Levitts. "All civilized people clothe themselves for decency, sir!"

"Not in my house," Dinky snapped back. "Even if the little doggie is watching, everyone in my house wanders in and out of the bathroom and they let it all-hang-out!"

Mary Daniels and Daisy were shocked at this remark, but Clyde laughed along with the others in the gallery. Once again, Judge Levitts banged his gavel. More sweat was pouring from his forehead and he was trying hard to keep his composure.

"I will have your last name, sir!" he commanded. "What was your father's last name?"

Dinky remained calm. "I never knew my father."

"Then what was your mother's name?"

"Sheba."

"Sheba...*what*?"

"Sheba...*down*!"

The crowd roared with laughter.

Judge Levitts picked up the pile of documents in front of him and slammed them down on the bench. "I will have quiet in my courtroom!" he bellowed.

The room fell silent again, and Judge Levitts tried to calm down.

"You never knew your father. Fine! I understand sir. I sympathize. But you had a father and he had a last name. A name he gave you by the fact of his own birth. What was that last name?"

"I heard about a name he used ..."

"Splendid. What was the name he used?"

"Well, it's kind of a silly name."

"A name is a name, sir! Repeat it."

"Okay. Wiggles."

Judge Levitts did not hear clearly, and he leaned over towards Dinky.

"What? What was that name?"

"Wiggles!"

"Woggles?"

"*Wiggles!*" shouted Dinky.

"Wiggles?"

"Yes! Yes! Wiggles!"

Judge Levitts then rose to his feet in triumph. He finally had his answer. He waved his gavel to the crowd to celebrate his victory over the bow-legged criminal in front of him.

"Then you're *Dinky Wiggles*!" he shouted.

"Not since the operation!" Dinky shouted back.

As the gallery roared, Judge Levitts smashed his gavel and it broke in two.

"Throw this man in jail!" he bellowed to the police. "Let him rot!"

Daisy Daniels now stood up and pointed to Dinky.

"He took my Dinky!" she sobbed. "He kidnapped my precious Dinky!"

Two policemen now rushed forward and grabbed Dinky and started to haul him away.

"I'm a dog!" Dinky yelled, as he was dragged out of the courtroom. "I despise that kid! I'm a dog! You will all see tonight! You will all be witnesses to the truth! Lemme go! I'm a dog!"

The police were able to force Dinky out the side door, but he grabbed the door frame and he was able to pop his head back into the open doorway long enough for one last, desperate yell.

"I'm a doggggggggggggg!"

Everyone in the courtroom could hear Dinky screaming as he was dragged out of the building. There was a loud slam of the main doors, and then silence.

"That Dinky-man is crazy," Judge Levitts said to the prosecutor. "I...I need one of my pills."

Suddenly, there was another voice in the courtroom that came from the last row of the gallery.

"I must speak now!" the voice thundered.

All attention was now turned to the back of the courtroom. A bald man with round, wire framed glasses stood up and surveyed the room. He had an absurdly long, thin face, like the face of an Alsatian Wolfhound without the fur. His head seemed about twice the size for a normal human body, and it hung out in front of him on a skinny vulture-neck. This made his whole body look like it was ready to tip forward and fall over under its own curious gravity.

Before he spoke, the strange man raised his hand and pointed to the ceiling, as if this gesture would give emphasis to what he was about to say.

The prosecutor turned to Judge Levitts. "That's Dr. Lothar Pettkus, the state-appointed psychiatrist."

"I'm a doctor!" Dr. Pettkus shouted in his thick Slavic accent, "And, I know this case!"

"Sir, you will remain silent in my courtroom!" Judge Levitts shouted back.

Dr. Pettkus would not be silenced. "There's only one cure for this strain of dementia!"

"Bailiff, remove that man!" commanded Judge Levitts.

"One cure! And that cure is...the *pound*!"

No one had a clue what this meant. The pound? The people in the courtroom knew of only one such place. Certainly, this outlandish man could not be talking about that dreadful dog-prison in the middle of Happy Valley Harbor.

Chapter 4
(24 Dog Hours)

Clyde Daniels and his family waited patiently by the main desk at the Happy Valley police station. They did not speak. Clyde looked very relaxed, but Mary Daniels looked blankly off into space and tapped her fingers nervously. Daisy read from one of her books, occasionally lowering the book from her eyes in order to study the clock on the wall near the desk. It was now 9:20 p.m.

Rex the police dog lay at the feet of the sergeant who was doing paperwork at the desk. Rex was also watching the clock. He made a low growling sound and gave the sergeant's leg a little nudge with his nose. The sergeant looked up at the clock.

"Well, now," he said. "Thanks, buddy-boy!"

The desk sergeant flicked a switch on the intercom in front of him and spoke in a commanding voice: "The prisoner will be brought into the main area, please."

Everyone now looked in the direction of Dinky's cell. He soon appeared in handcuffs, being led by two policemen who followed close behind him. As soon as Daisy saw him she gave a frightened whimper and inched closer to her mother.

"It's all right, sweetheart," her mother whispered, patting Daisy lightly on the cheek.

"Take the cuffs off," the sergeant said.

Dinky's handcuffs were quickly removed, and he stretched his arms.

"Okay, pal," the sergeant said. "Beats the heck outta me what you're gonna do now, but you produce the dog like you promised and the family here is gonna drop the charges. So?"

Everyone waited. Dinky looked at the clock. It was not quite 9:30. Dinky turned and faced the Daniels family.

"It is not yet 9:30. I will produce your little dog at 9:30 precisely!" Dinky now looked directly at Clyde. "I began this sad adventure as a miserable ugly mutt. And I go back to the creature I was with one blessing. And that is the blessing of wisdom, and the peace of mind that goes with wisdom. Mr. Daniels, I won first prize for being the World's Ugliest Mutt, because like it or not, that's exactly what I am!"

The second hand of the clock now swept up to the top and it was 9:30 exactly. All of the staff at the police station had gathered around the desk to watch, and they quietly snickered to themselves.

"We will see who laughs last, you pinheads!" shouted Dinky. He then crossed his arms and stomped on the floor. "I use my wish to become a dog again!"

Dinky stood rigid after this pronouncement, and everyone leaned forward. No one spoke.

They all waited for something to happen. But nothing at all happened. After a few seconds, Dinky tried again.

"I said, *I wish to become an ugly mutt again! That is my wish! Amen!"*

Again, Dinky stomped on the floor. But again, nothing happened.

"I know!" Dinky shouted, "We have to be outside! To speak to a higher power, you gotta speak waaaay up to the heavens!"

****

The group was now gathered in front of the police station. A few people passing by on the sidewalk had stopped to watch. Dinky puffed up his chest and raised his arms up as high as they would go. He steadied himself, then began to shout up to the night sky.

"Oh, great God of all dogs, hear me! Let thy humble servant Dinky be a dog again. That is my wish, and it is written in the stars!"

A flash of lightning now burst through the night sky, followed by a boom of thunder. The heavens were about to open wide and reveal the secrets of the Universe, but instead all Dinky got was a miserable sprinkle of rain that fell directly onto his face. Flustered now, he pointed to the clock tower at the nearby city hall. It was now several minutes after 9:30.

"Don't the stupid clocks work in this town?" Dinky yelled.

Then a voice rose up from the sidewalk. "She gave you 24 dog hours, moron."

"Who said that?" demanded Dinky.

Rex now slipped out between the legs of the waiting policemen. He had a deadpan expression, and he spoke with a droll British accent.

"24 dog hours is a whole week of human time. Welcome to the real world, Dinky."

"A week?" shouted Dinky.

"Well you do get credit for the last 24 hours, and the clock is always ticking, so..."

"That's impossible!"

"I see. You are really a dog made human by an angel. You and I are having a conversation no one else can hear. But everything else is impossible. Wonderful."

Dinky rushed up to Rex and crouched down low on the sidewalk.

"A week? Rex, if I have to spend another week..."

"Six days, Dinky. Aren't you listening?"

"Six more days of this and I'm gonna go ape - !"

"Dinky!" Rex interrupted, stone-faced and impassive. "If you want to win friends and influence people, discussing your own sanity nose-to-nose with a dog is not a good start. The use of profanity is also highly inappropriate, and screaming it all at the top of your lungs is even worse."

Rex then glanced upwards.

"I said that no one could hear us, but that was what they call a half-truth. The whole truth is, they can only hear half the conversation. Me, I'm just a stupid dog."

Dinky slowly rose to his feet and looked around at the crowd that had gathered in front of him.

"Hey folks..." Dinky stammered, "This isn't what it seems."

One of the policemen slowly approached Dinky with the handcuffs.

"Now you just settle down, Dinky-man," the policeman smiled. "We'll get you back where it's warm and dry and fix you up with a couple of nice Benny Bully Pork Yummies!"

A thought now flashed through Dinky's mind.

"Hey, wait a minute!" he shouted. "24 dog hours? That's not a week! It's only 3.42 hours of human time!"

"Not true," said the policeman with the handcuffs. "A human must go 7 days to experience the aging equivalent of a dog in 24 hours! Come here, boy!"

Six year old Henry Beamish, the town genius, now burst out of the crowd.

"You are both wrong!" Henry exclaimed, excitedly. "You have both reached the same conclusion in the absence of any empirical data."

"They are not the same, Henry," an old lady said. "Each theory has its own statistical variation."

The whole crowd then broke into a heated argument about dog-years and no one seemed to notice Dinky any more. Even the policeman with the handcuffs was yelling furiously at young Henry Beamish about dog-time and dog-hours and dog-everything-else. Dinky took a few steps back from this strangely animated mob and shook his head.

"Humans," he muttered.

Then, Dinky turned and ran as fast as he could down the street.

"Hey!" someone yelled. "He's getting away!"

The crowd ran after Dinky with Rex leading the chase.

Dinky cut into a side street, then took a quick turn down a narrow alley that ran behind the city hall. He thought he had made his escape, but a few seconds later Rex appeared at the alley entrance. Dinky could hear the sounds of the policemen coming up fast.

Rex looked straight at Dinky. He could have nabbed him in an instant. But Rex waited a moment, then continued to run straight ahead down the side street.

The policeman soon followed Rex down the street and they all hurried past the alley without looking.

Now alone in the alley, Dinky paused to catch his breath. He could hear the sounds of the police chase fading away in the distance. There was a long pause and Dinky was aware of his own heavy breathing. All was still and silent for a few moments. Then Dinky was startled by the sound of Rex's voice directly behind him.

"I don't want you to panic," said Rex in his calm monotone. "Just turn around very slowly."

Dinky turned and faced Rex. He noticed the shadowy figures of some other dogs behind Rex near the alley entrance.

"They won't harm you," Rex said. "We have a couple of minutes alone before all the flatfoots arrive."

Rex then gave a low whistle and Dinky watched the other dogs move towards them.

"They're homeless dogs," Rex explained. "I slip 'em a bit of food when I can, try to help them out. Come on, guys! Dinky's all right. He's just one of those poor suckers who got what he wished for."

The other dogs reached Dinky and Rex. They were friendly dogs, and they wagged their tails as they gathered around. The lead dog was an old dog with grey whiskers and a warm smile. Dinky knelt down and gave him a hug.

"My name is Sparks, but they call me Old Sparky," the old dog said. "I guess you could say that I lead this gang of ruffians."

In the distance, they could all hear shouting and the piercing sound of a police whistle.

"They're gonna get you one way or the other," said Old Sparky. "Ya can't run and hide like we all do."

"You just follow me, Dinky," said Rex. "I walk ahead, you keep close. Two steps back, no further. Understood?"

Dinky understood. Rex led him back down the alley towards the side street. The other dogs followed at a safe distance. When Rex reached the end of the alley, he stopped and turned to Dinky.

"You gotta go back to the police station, Dinky," Rex said. "I'll help you get through this, but no funny stuff. You run again, and I'll bite your butt so hard you won't be able to sit down for a week. Nothing personal, mind you. Just doing my job."

"Rex, I'm scared," said Dinky. His voice was trembling.

A small dog broke from the group and ran up to Dinky.

"Hey, Dinky," the small dog said, "Word on the street is, they're gonna turn you over to the mad doctor! Toss you into the dog pound!"

"What...what doctor?" said Dinky. He was so scared he could hardly speak.

"Could you look out for my buddy Penny?" the little dog asked. "She's gone missing."

"Let's go!" said Rex. "I mean, *now*."

Rex took the lead and Dinky followed two steps behind exactly as Rex had ordered. The other dogs stayed back in the alley as Rex led Dinky back down the street towards the police station.

"I have a good life here," Rex said cheerfully as they went along. "I bite the odd shoplifter on the butt and the police love me for it. I'm not throwing it away on you or any other dog in shoe leather. Cheer up, Dinky! It's only six more days. You want a laugh? There's this dog, see, and he's driving around in his car.

47

What's he looking for? A barking space! Ha! Ha! I thought that was a good one."

Dinky wasn't laughing. He followed Rex along the walkway towards the police station, then up the short flight of stairs to the main door. Rex gave the door a little bump with his nose and the door slowly opened. They went inside, with Rex in the lead and Dinky following two steps behind, just like he was told.

Inside the station, the sergeant at the desk stood up and tossed Rex a biscuit.

"Good boy, Rex!" the sergeant smiled.

The other policemen now burst through the open door. They were gasping for breath and almost doubled over with exhaustion.

"We were right on top of him sir," one of them said.

The desk sergeant turned to Dinky. "I see trouble coming up at six o'clock there, pal. Right behind ya!"

Dinky did not know what this meant. He spun around on his heels and suddenly came face to face with the foreboding and all-too-menacing figure of Dr. Lothar Pettkus, M.D.

"Ahhhhh!" Dinky gasped. He had never seen such a strange looking human.

"Ahhhhh!" Dr. Pettkus yelled in the same instant.

Something about Dinky the man-dog was not quite right, either.

"Meet Dr. Pettkus, Dinky," the desk sergeant said. "We all know you're a whacko, but next to Dr. Pettkus you're a poster boy for sanity."

The other policemen laughed at this remark, but Dr. Pettkus frowned and his eyes seemed to sink further back into their sockets.

"I will have you know I attended the Blitnik Academy in Budapest," he sneered. "That's a far cry from the Happy Valley Police Academy, don't you think?"

"Oh, I've had way more education than that, Doc," said the desk sergeant. "I was at Harvard."

This stopped Dr. Pettkus in his tracks. It was like a chorus of angels had rung through the building. Harvard! He was at a loss for words.

"You were at *Harvard*?" Dr. Pettkus stammered, trying hard to hide his envy.

"Sure," said the desk sergeant. "Those washrooms have never been cleaner!"

Dr. Pettkus was a man with zero sense of humor. He looked at Dinky and snapped his fingers. "I wish to be alone with the patient," he barked.

****

Dinky soon found himself back in his cell. Dr. Pettkus stood on the other side of the cell bars. He rubbed his chin with his bony fingers and studied Dinky for a long time. Dinky sat on the bed and stared back at him. He had only met Dr. Pettkus five minutes ago, yet there was something about this bizarre human that turned his dog-blood to ice.

The two of them locked eyes for a long time. Finally, Dr. Pettkus spoke.

"Now, Danky..."

"It's Dinky!"

"Din-key! Fine. Danky..."

"Dinky!"

"You seem to be on this strange crusade to convince others you are something you are not."

Dinky put his feet up on the bed and made a sudden barking sound. Dr. Pettkus jumped back, and then broke into a nervous grin.

"Ohhhh, good one! You think you got me, huh?"

Dinky stretched out on the bed and put his arms behind his head. "Doc, just have them feed me for a few more days, will you? It's scary out there!"

This time, Dr. Pettkus made sure he was pronouncing Dinky's name correctly.

"Now...*Dinky*," he began, "If you *are* a dog, then tell me why a dog always goes back to his master?"

"Beats me," said Dinky, looking up at the ceiling.

Dr. Pettkus seemed intent on getting an answer to this odd question.

"But dogs know!" he exclaimed. "People say: 'I have a dog of a car!' or 'I had a dog of a day!' or 'I have a dog of a pain right-in-my-butt!' Do you see? Infinite cruelty and disrespect! But the loyal dog, the friend of man, he returns to the master again and again."

Now, Dr. Pettkus pressed close to the cell bars.

"If you're a real dog, you'd know the answer. Tell me why!"

"A dog needs the love of his master," Dinky said.

"Yes, but why?"

"Without the love of his master, the dog won't exist."

Dr. Pettkus was stunned. His eyes widened and he stepped back from the cell bars and glared at Dinky.

Dinky said nothing more and continued to stare up at the ceiling. It was like the words he had just spoken had no special meaning to him at all.

After all, didn't everyone know that a dog is just a puff of smoke without the love of his master?

Chapter 5
(The Blind Man)

The interrogation room at the Happy Valley police station was barely big enough for the table and two chairs they had crammed into it. Dinky sat with a nurse in a white uniform who was showing him a series of drawings and asking him to comment on each one. Dinky had been human for a couple of days now, and he wanted nothing more to do with lawyers and courtrooms and he especially wanted nothing more to do with Judge Levitts. He would remain in the comfortable jail until it was all over. The angel had been right all along, of course. One wish, and he would never make another wish for the rest of his life.

The nurse handed Dinky a drawing of a family out for a drive with their dog driving the car.

"What's wrong with this picture, Dinky?" the nurse asked.

Dinky pointed to the dog.

"Very good!" the nurse exclaimed. "I think you're coming along just fine."

"No seatbelt," Dinky said.

In the next room, Dr. Pettkus and two other doctors were watching Dinky through the one-way glass. The two other doctors were laughing, but Dr. Pettkus was dead serious. He pressed his face to the glass and frowned.

"That guy's funny," said one of the doctors.

"Here's one my kid told me last night," said the other doctor. "Where did the dog go when he lost his tail? The retail store!"

The two doctors cracked up, but Dr. Pettkus did not change his expression. He continued to stare through the one-way mirror.

"This is no time for a joke," he muttered. "The patient is sick. He suffers from Canine Dementia."

"Pettkus, 1 bet you're a barrel of laughs on amateur night down at Yuk-Yuk's," said the doctor who had told the joke. "Sheesh! Lighten up!"

"Your crackpot theories are getting on everybody's nerves," said the other doctor. "Canine Dementia! What a load of horse crap."

Dr. Pettkus was insulted. "I completed my doctoral thesis on Canine Dementia at the Blitnik Academy in Budapest!" he said. "I achieved a grade of B minus."

"It's *still* horse crap," the other doctor said. "And I never heard of the Blitnik Academy."

"Shut up, you two," said the first doctor. "I think he's sane enough to be let out."

Dr. Pettkus grabbed the first doctor by the lapels of his jacket and pulled him so close so they were almost face to face. The doctor struggled to move away, but Dr. Pettkus held on tight.

"Noooo!" Dr. Pettkus insisted. "There is only one cure for Canine Dementia! And that's total social immersion with the species that acts as the foundation for the delusion. With total immersion the patient gains awareness into the symptomatology that simple logic cannot provide. And, with such awareness comes insight. And, with insight, the patient is cured. The pound is the only answer! The pound!"

A feverish Dr. Pettkus now let go and the doctor fell back and stumbled into the first doctor. The two of them stared at Dr. Pettkus. He had always looked strange, but now his nose seemed longer and wider than ever, and his smooth face had the beginnings of a light fur growing all over. Perhaps he had forgotten to shave that morning.

****

A few minutes later, Dinky found himself facing the desk sergeant in the main area of the police station. Dinky was now wearing proper clothing that had been left for him on the station steps by an anonymous donor. He was uncomfortable in this strange human clothing, and he kept putting his weight on one foot, then the other. He was still a little shaky on his feet, and he tried to steady himself by holding onto the desk.

"Still weaving like a drunk, huh?" asked the sergeant. "Well, it ain't our problem anymore, thank goodness. I hear it was a two to one split, but you're free to go."

"Go where?" Dinky asked, puzzled. "I like it here. I'm hungry and I don't know where to go!"

"Try the nuthouse," said the sergeant. "Scram, buddy!"

"The nuthouse?"

"Get outta here!"

A policeman dragged Dinky away from the desk and pushed him out of the station. The door slammed behind him, and Dinky found himself in the middle of a typical busy day on the streets of Happy Valley. He didn't know what to do. He stumbled down the stairs to the sidewalk, then paused to look around. People hurried by him and traffic rushed up and down the noisy street. Dinky was starving, and he tried to get the attention of someone who might help him out. He gave a big wave to an Amish man who approached.

"Hello, I'm a dog!" Dinky said with a friendly smile, "And I wanna go to the nuthouse!"

But the Amish man just kept walking, and no one else seemed to hear him. In fact, nobody paid any attention at all.

Dinky took a few more steps and he was soon swept along with the movement of the others on the sidewalk. He tried to ask for help, but it was useless. No one stopped. No one even listened. As he wobbled along on his new human legs, he noticed up ahead of him a blind man standing on the street corner with a dog beside him. The dog was in a leather harness with a leash that ran from the harness and looped around the blind man's white cane.

The blind man clutched the cane in one hand, and held a tin cup in his other hand. The tin cup had a few coins in it, and as people passed by him the blind man would shake his hand and the coins would rattle around in the bottom of the cup. The blind man sensed Dinky's presence as he approached.

"Friend!" the blind man exclaimed, with a wide smile. He held out the cup and rattled the coins. "Help out a poor blind beggar and his starving dog?"

"I'm starving too, and I would like some food to eat, kind sir," Dinky said politely.

The blind man's expression suddenly hardened.

"You want something to eat?" he exclaimed. "You can eat my shorts! The only other mouth I'm feeding today is my good buddy, King. Get outta here ya welfare bum! Get a job!"

The blind man thrashed his cane in Dinky's direction, but Dinky quickly stepped back as the cane swished through the air. Dinky paused, then slowly crept up to the blind man's dog and quickly released the harness. The dog trotted happily down the sidewalk.

Dinky then slipped the harness over his own head and got down on all fours beside the blind man. He had done this so carefully and so swiftly that the blind man had not felt a thing.

Just as Dinky crouched down on the pavement to start begging with the blind man, someone walked by and tossed a coin into the blind man's tin cup.

"Thank you! Thank you, sir!" exclaimed the blind man, now all excited. He grabbed the coin and ran his fingers over the surface. His expression fell.

"A nickel?" the blind man shouted. "Why, you cheap - !"

The sudden sound of a honking car horn drowned out the blind man's last word. But Dinky was close enough to hear the word he used. He had heard the word before, and he had almost used it himself in his first conversation with Rex outside the police station last night. It was an adjective, a human-type word that described a person, place, or thing. Often used in anger, too.

"We'll eat today, King boy," the blind man said, "Don't you worry. Nice boy. Nice dog!"

The blind man reached down to pat his dog. Dinky extended his head, and the blind man gently stroked his hair. "Oh, King boy," the blind man said sadly. "I gotta get you to the dog groomers. We both need a haircut bad! Poor thing."

The blind man now took something out of his pocket that looked like a piece of floppy rubber.

"Here's a nice treat for you, King boy," he said. "My last slice of cow brain!"

Dinky took this revolting treat in his mouth and gagged it down. At least it was something to keep him from falling over dead from hunger. As he gulped the last bit of cow brain, an old lady walked by pushing a shopping cart.

"I don't think that's funny at all," the old lady said to the blind man.

"You and me both, lady," the blind man responded. "I'm blind and you're ugly!"

Another lady now walked by, holding her young daughter by the hand.

"I really like your dog, blind man," said the girl. "It's *sooo avant-garde*. You a performance artist or something?"

"Up yours, kid!" shouted the blind man.

"Don't talk to strangers!" said the girl's mother, pulling her away.

Again, the blind man swished the air violently with his cane.

"One of these days I'm gonna knock one of those snob goombahs right out into the street!" he shouted. "What is it with people nowadays, King boy? They don't respect nothin'. Come on, boy – we know when we're not wanted! This corner sucks!"

The blind man took a big yank on the dog leash and stepped right out into the busy four-lane street. He started tap-tap-tapping furiously on the pavement as he went along.

Dinky had no choice but to scamper on all fours ahead of him and lead the way. The street now rang with the sounds of screeching brakes and honking horns and smashing metal. Still, the blind man kept tap-tap-tapping boldly along, paying no attention whatsoever to the chaos and destruction he was causing. Dinky was terrified, certain that the next moment would be his last.

"My whole life I been poor!" screamed the blind man, as he tap-tap-tapped his way through all the noise and flying auto parts. "I was born poor, dirt poor. Pukingly poor! When I was a kid, all the other blind kids had Seeing Eye dogs. My old man gave me a Seeing Eye cockroach! Oh, King – I've been praying all my life for that one big break that will make my fortune. That moment when God Almighty reaches down from Heaven and says: 'Here, Blind Billy, you suffered long enough ya dumb schmuck. Here's a zillion bucks!' I know that moment's comin' King, boy. But when? When's my ship comin' in?"

At that moment, Judge Levitts was driving his car towards Dinky and the blind man, but he didn't yet realize what was happening in front of him. His wife sat beside him, talking a mile a minute. Judge Levitts was doing his best to listen to her, but his mind was elsewhere.

"And then that Dorothy McGillicuddy..." Mrs. Levitts said. "She had the nerve to tell me, right in front of the others...*watch where you're driving, pig brain*!"

Judge Levitts looked at his wife, waiting for her to continue her story. As he turned his eyes back to the road, he saw an oncoming semi-trailer rig headed straight for him. His face froze and he slammed on the brakes.

Dinky and the blind man had now reached the other side of the street.

"When's Blind Billy's ship comin' in?" the blind man continued to rave. "When's all my dreams comin' true? Ya gotta have heart! Ya gotta have hope!"

Smashed vehicles and injured drivers were scattered everywhere, but Dinky and the blind man took their last few steps and reached the other sidewalk without a scratch. It was a miracle! Dinky couldn't believe that he'd lived through it all. He was so swept up in all the blind man's positive talk and so happy to be alive that he stood up from his crouched doggie-squat and spread his arms out wide.

"That's right!" Dinky shouted, beaming with eternal hope. "Ya gotta keep walking that street of dreams!"

The blind man stopped dead in his tracks and his jaw dropped. You could almost hear the sound of a cash register ringing in his ears.

"A talking dog!" he exclaimed with a greedy smile.

The blind man then pulled violently on the dog leash, which caused Dinky to lurch forward and smash his head into a nearby lamp post. Dinky crumpled slowly to the sidewalk, knocked out cold.

****

Dr. Pettkus was taking his morning walk down Main Street. He muttered to himself as he walked along, making sure he didn't step on any of the sidewalk cracks. Some of the people who passed by him tended to stare at him, but that was nothing new for Dr. Pettkus. He was used to people being startled by his strange appearance, and he paid no attention.

But something ahead of him did attract his interest. There was a large crowd gathered on the sidewalk around a lamp post and Dr. Pettkus could hear shouting and the wailing of approaching police sirens. He then noticed that the street around him was scattered with smashed cars, and when he took another step he had to avoid a car bumper that had tumbled onto the sidewalk.

Dr. Pettkus pushed his way through the crowd. He looked down and saw Dinky lying on the sidewalk by the lamp post, all tangled up in the leash and the dog harness. Dinky was groggy and just regaining consciousness. He did not speak.

"Ah!" said Dr. Pettkus. "The patient!"

Dr. Pettkus then heard the cries of the blind man a few feet away. The blind man was standing at the corner cigar store, and he was shouting at the imposing figure of a brightly painted cigar store Indian on the sidewalk just outside the front door of the shop. As he shouted at the wooden statue, he kept beating it over the head with his white cane. The Indian held a bunch of cigars in his clenched fist, and he used his other hand with its long, carved fingers to shield his eyes as he surveyed the rolling landscape in front of him.

"You were never a father to me and now you're speechless!" ranted the blind man to the statue, whacking it repeatedly over the head. "You're still a socialist hypocrite and I'm rich! I'm a

61

zillionaire! A trillionaire! King will tell ya! Tell him, King boy! Tell poor dumb-dumb-democrat poppa that Blind Billy's ship has finally come in to port!"

The blind man gave the statue one more whack with the cane, and the head broke from its support and toppled over. Terrified now, the blind man dropped to his knees and groped around the sidewalk for the severed head.

"Poppa! Poppa!" the blind man cried. "I killed poor poppa!"

Dinky started to moan. At that moment, Judge Levitts appeared on the sidewalk, stumbling towards the little group that surrounded Dinky. He was dazed and bleeding, and had the steering wheel of his car wrapped around his neck. Dr. Pettkus gave Judge Levitts a big smile of triumph. He then grabbed the steering wheel and twisted Judge Levitt's head around so his eyes were pointing directly at poor Dinky on the sidewalk beneath them.

"I'm a dog. I'm a dog!" Dinky began to moan.

"You see?" beamed Dr. Pettkus. He yanked the judge's head around even further, and forced him to look down. "Look for yourself! Death and destruction everywhere! And why? The patient needs the cure!"

Then Dr. Pettkus let go of the steering wheel and Judge Levitts fell on top of Dinky in a heap. Dr. Pettkus stepped back and addressed the bewildered crowd.

"The pound, I tell all of you!" he yelled. "The pound! *The dog pound*!"

Chapter 6
(Dog-Alcatraz)

The Happy Valley dog pound was located on a small island in the middle of Happy Valley Harbor. The pound was built in 1939 under the supervision of a local veterinarian named Edward Booth. Dr. Booth always claimed to love the animals he treated, but he was stubbornly of the view that a stray dog had to be a runaway dog. He thought the best way to handle such dogs was to put them in prison as a deterrent for any future runaway behavior. The fact that most stray dogs were born that way did not seem to impress Dr. Booth.

He designed his dog pound after the real Alcatraz prison in San Francisco, and he ran it just like a real prison, with high walls, armed guards – and an execution chamber for any dog that lasted longer than a week without being adopted. Dr. Booth developed a bit of a cult following in the early days, and it was even rumored that a few more dog-prisons had sprung up around the country as a tribute to his unique methodology.

Dr. Booth had a lot of weird ideas when it came to animals. He claimed he could channel the spirits of his dead pets, and he was especially grief-stricken when his favorite parrot, Laszlo, keeled over and died unexpectedly of a heart attack. Convinced that he could summon Laszlo's spirit into his own body, Dr. Booth took a trip to New York and jumped off the Empire State building in a vain attempt to prove his theory. Unfortunately, all he was able to prove was that a falling body from a great height falls very fast indeed.

After his death, Dr. Booth was quickly forgotten. Had the citizens of Happy Valley had a slightly longer memory, they might have questioned some of Dr. Booth's crazy animal theories and built a proper home for their stray dogs. But the prison had remained in operation year after year, and over those years many a sorry dog had taken a one-way trip to the grimy, crumbling walls of Dog-Alcatraz.

****

Dinky was seated in the little boat under the watchful eye of two prison guards. He was handcuffed to an iron bench which was then bolted onto the floor of the boat. Ahead of him, the towering walls of Dog-Alcatraz loomed up huge in the darkness. There was a light rain that night, and the fog was rolling in. Dinky watched as the prison walls grew larger and larger, and the darkness and the fog made it all unbearably gloomy.

Beside him in the little boat sat Dr. Pettkus. The two of them bounced on the waves in silence. As they reached the prison dock, Dr. Pettkus nodded towards the huge stone walls that now seemed to rise up to the stars.

"Do we like our new home, Danky?" Dr. Pettkus asked with a sly smile.

Dinky just hung his head and didn't respond.

Dinky was led off the boat down a long walkway and into the prison courtyard. He had two guards on either side of him, and Dr. Pettkus followed close behind. They crossed the courtyard and entered the main prison through a huge stone archway that rose up high above their heads. The guards led Dinky through a narrow stone corridor that led up to another guard who sat on a chair beside a locked door with long metal bars. Through the bars, Dinky could see the huge cell block at the far end of the building that contained all the dog-prisoners.

"Prisoner delivered!" said one of the guards. The two guards then turned around and left.

Dr. Pettkus then stepped forward and handed a document to the guard at the gate.

"This is the court order," said Dr. Pettkus. "The prisoner will be held in the cells and he'll be moved in rotation with the other dogs."

As the prison guard read the court order, Dinky noticed Rex the police dog behind the door with the bars. Rex looked at him and

65

gave a sly wink. The guard handed the court order back to Dr. Pettkus, and unlocked the door. Dinky and Dr. Pettkus went inside, and the guard slammed the door shut again.

"I will take the prisoner to his cell," Dr. Pettkus said. The guard didn't argue.

As soon as they got inside, Rex trotted up to Dinky and gave him a little bark. This startled Dr. Pettkus, who abruptly stopped walking.

"He's a sweetheart, don't worry!" yelled the guard from the other side of the door.

Rex then looked at Dr. Pettkus and gave another friendly bark. He held up his paw.

Dr. Pettkus forced a thin smile. He did not like dogs. "Shake a paw, boy! He's a friendly one, is he?"

Dr. Pettkus reluctantly shook Rex's paw, and Rex gave him a couple of friendly little dog squeals. As Dr. Pettkus led Dinky towards his cell, Rex trotted behind them. As they walked, Dinky was aware that all the dog-prisoners were watching him silently from their own cells. Some of the prisoners sat on the floor like dogs. Others stood up and hung their paws through their cell bars. Still others lay on their beds, motionless. But they were all watching, and no one made a sound.

"I'm right behind you, Dinky," Rex said. "That stupid quack doctor can't hear a thing."

Dinky looked at Dr. Pettkus. He walked straight ahead, as if a talking police dog behind him was the very last thing on his mind.

Dinky started to speak, then he stopped abruptly. "Rex, I'm not sure..."

"He can't hear you either, Dinky. No one listens, and no one cares."

"What are you doing here?" Dinky asked, as Dr. Pettkus led him down the long cell block.

"Oh, I moonlight a bit," Rex said casually. "Pick up an extra buck when I can. Costs a fortune to put six kids through obedience school, you know."

When they approached Dinky's cell, Rex stopped. "I'll do the best I can to keep an eye on you. Remember, five days!"

Rex turned and went back to the guard at the door. By then, Dr. Pettkus had led Dinky all the way down the cell block to an empty cell at the far end. This cell was nothing like his cozy cell at the police station. This was a dark, narrow, hole-in-the-wall, like something from a medieval stone dungeon. There was no furniture, just two bunk-style beds fastened to one wall.

Dinky noticed an empty doggie dish in one corner. There was a barred window high above the bunk-beds, and a little moonlight streamed through the window and illuminated the grey stone floor and some scattered bits of straw.

Dr. Pettkus kicked the door open and craned his vulture-neck so his head stuck out even further. "Inside! Go-go-go-go! Danky!"

Dinky had no choice. He stepped into the dreary room and Dr. Pettkus slammed the door behind him. "I'd like a few moments alone with the prisoner!" Dr. Pettkus shouted to the guard at the gate.

The guard was reading a book on his Kindle, and he didn't answer. Dr. Pettkus now studied Dinky as Dinky inspected his new surroundings.

"Cat got your tongue, Danky?" Dr. Pettkus asked.

Dinky did not respond. He took a step towards the cell bars, but Dr. Pettkus did not retreat.

"How do we like our new room, Danky?"

Dinky still didn't respond.

"How do we like our new bed?"

Dinky said nothing.

"Now Danky..."

Suddenly, Dinky lunged forward. In the same motion, he reached through the cell bars and grabbed Dr. Pettkus by the throat, pulling him forward and ramming his face into the bars.

"It's *Dinkyyyy*!" Dinky screamed at Dr. Pettkus as he squeezed with all his might.

Dr. Pettkus turned purple and his eyes bulged, but he remained strangely calm.

"Now, Danky," Dr. Pettkus squeaked, "If you are a dog, then something made you human without taking away your past! Will you use your wish to erase your past from your memory? What then? Would you still hear the whispered voices? And the howling? The incessant torment? 'The wish has been wasted, and the only thing left to take you back, is your own *madness*!' Bad dog!"

Dinky released his grip and Dr. Pettkus stumbled backwards. Clutching his throat and gasping for breath, he staggered back down the corridor between the cells towards the guard at the gate. The other dog-prisoners watched him, staring silently as they had done with Dinky. The guard opened the gate, and Dr. Pettkus slipped quickly into the night. There was the sound of the gate closing again, and then silence.

Dinky slumped down on the bottom bunk of his cell and looked up at the moonlight coming through the small window. Muffled dog-sounds now came drifting from the walkway into his cell. These were indistinct sounds at first, but as the sounds they grew louder they transformed into the clear voices of the other prisoners.

"Hey! Hey new guy! You're no human!"

"What gives, stranger?"

"You in for the Big Ride in seven days?"

"You better get a refund on that return ticket to town!"

This made all the dog-prisoners laugh with a strange bark-laugh that echoed through the building. Through it all, the guard at the door kept reading his Kindle. He had heard nothing.

Dinky summoned the courage to speak. "What's the Big Ride?" he asked nervously.

No one answered. Dinky waited in silence, but there were no more voices. Then he heard another voice from coming beneath a pile of straw at the corner of the cell.

69

"The Big Ride is what you get a week from now if nobody adopts you," said the voice.

Dinky leaned forward, and saw Penny emerge from the straw and step into the stream of moonlight. She shook the bits of straw off her body and gave Dinky a big smile.

"You!" exclaimed Dinky.

"Here I was, warning you about this place and now we end up as cell mates!" Penny said. "If I had any kind of an education, I would call that 'dramatic irony' and end up with an A+ on my term paper!"

Dinky looked down at the little dog, now smiling up at him. He remembered her from the parking lot at the jail, but he now had a chance to have a good look at her. He had never seen a dog before that even remotely resembled his old doggie-self.

"Goodness," said Penny, "Am I that ugly?"

"You look like a person I know," said Dinky.

"You mean, I look like you," Penny corrected him. "Don't dance around the truth, Dinky. It doesn't suit you, and it's bad manners. Can you pick me up?"

Dinky reached down and scooped Penny up and cradled her in his arms. She was a sweet little creature, comfortable with her own ugliness and happy in her dank surroundings. She was not at all sorry for herself. She looked up at Dinky and grinned.

"Rex spread the word about you," Penny said. "He's the best friend on the outside any of us could have. He knows I'm here, but I told him not to worry Old Sparky and the others. I used to run with that bunch. They were like family. Heck, they *were* my family! But I let myself get caught by the flatfoots and get tossed into this joint. I got tired of hiding out at the dog park during the day, and running at night from all those awful headlights! And I was lonely in that big old warehouse! If no one wants to adopt me, well I figure that must be part of God's plan."

Dinky held Penny closer, and she gave him a shy smile.

"Penny, what happens in here after seven days?" he asked.

"That's not something you have to worry about," Penny said, "Because you're getting out in five days. All my pals at the dog park would sure get a kick out of you!"

Dinky thought about this. "Dr. Pettkus thinks this place will bring me to my senses. I can get out of here now if I tell him I'm not a dog."

Penny looked at him thoughtfully. "You cried yourself to sleep when you were a dog. But you still had a roof over your head and a full stomach. Now, you look like a person and you tell people you're a dog, and presto! Same thing happens. Roof over your head and three square a day. Take the dog out of the picture and where do you go? You go begging. Don't be angry with me, Dinky. I know I talk too much."

There was a long silence. "Could you put me down?" Penny asked.

Dinky placed Penny gently back on the floor. She took her paw and scratched some more straw on the pile, then curled up on the pile and closed her eyes. Dinky stared at her.

"You let yourself get tossed into this place, did you?" he asked quietly.

Penny yawned. "I wanna be more like my mother. She wasn't afraid of anything. Night, Dinky."

"Night."

Dinky waited until Penny had fallen asleep. Then he got up and stood at the cell bars, looking across at the other cells. The dog-prisoners were now asleep. All was silent for a moment, but the silence was quickly broken by the voice of a menacing looking prison guard who was doing his nightly rounds.

"Hands off the bars, dog-boy!" the guard warned.

Dinky stepped back. He was not going to create the slightest trouble for himself. It was only a few more days.

****

The next morning, Dinky was awakened by the sound of a family coming up the cell block corridor, inspecting all the dogs. By the sound of their excited voices, they were looking for a new pet. Dinky saw Penny nervously waiting by the cell bars, listening to the voices as they got closer.

The family reached Penny and stopped. They stared down at her. There was a pause, then there was some muffled laughter and they all kept walking. Penny did not react. But as they passed by, Penny's sad eyes followed them.

****

The exercise yard at Dog-Alcatraz was packed with every dog in the joint. It was an astonishing sight. There were dogs walking on two legs, and dogs walking on all fours. There were dogs in striped prison outfits, and dogs wearing nothing at all. The dog-prisoners were a blend of every style you could imagine, yet it all looked seamless and perfectly natural.

There were high guard towers overhead at each corner of the yard, and the guards in the towers looked bored. They fiddled with their radios and drank coffee. Beneath them was a buzzing dog community, but the guards paid no attention. They never did.

Penny led Dinky through the yard as the dog-prisoners stared at him.

"Don't sweat it, Dinky," Penny said, taking charge. "They all know who you are, and nobody's gonna hurt you as long as I'm around. Just be cool, be very cool."

"Hey, Penny!" one prisoner yelled.

"Hey, Butch!" Penny yelled back.

"Mornin' sweetheart!" another dog called out.

"You still in here, Sluggo?" Penny asked. "You just can't con that nasty parole board, now can ya?"

"Ha! That's a good one," the dog shot back.

Penny spotted another dog approaching them from the far end of the yard. This was a tough-looking dog, and he was followed by a group of dogs that stuck close behind him in a tight pack.

"Hey! There's my buddy, Spike!" said Penny. "He's the head dog in here. Hey, Spike!"

Spike was the head dog, there was no doubt about it. All the other dogs parted for him as he approached Dinky and Penny with his tough-dog buddies close on his heels. As he got closer, one of the dog prisoners ran up to him. This dog wore thick-rimmed glasses with tape in the middle.

"Morning, Spike," said Nerd Dog eagerly. "You have a good sleep, Spike? Anything I can do for ya, Spike? Can I hang with ya, Spike?"

Spike stopped walking and he gave Nerd Dog a long, hard look. He did not respond, and Nerd Dog slinked away. Spike quickly reached Penny, and he gave her a big kiss on the cheek.

"Morning, little sister," Spike said. "Ain't you been adopted yet?"

"All in good time, Spike," said Penny.

Spike then took a long look at Dinky. "You don't look like a dog to me, stranger," he said.

"Hey, don't give him a hard time, Spike," Penny said. "He's new here!"

"I think your new best friend can speak for himself, Penny," Spike said in a low growl.

The dogs all surrounded Dinky. He didn't know what to do.

"Tell us, Penny's new best friend," Spike continued. "Why doesn't a dog die of embarrassment every time his owner takes him for a walk and makes him squeeze out a steamer in broad daylight?"

"I can't answer for other dogs," Dinky said.

Spike pressed him. "What's your answer, friend?"

"I die of embarrassment every day," said Dinky.

"He *is* a dog!" exclaimed Spike.

This broke the tension, and the other dogs now started to chat with Penny. She was the center of attention. Dinky and Spike quickly found themselves together a few feet back from the group. There was an awkward silence between them. Dinky stared at a strange-looking gold name tag around Spike's neck.

"Penny's mother gave it to me," Spike said. "It's Latin. It means 'tough guy'. Sometimes I wonder."

This was a casual comment from the head prison dog, but in Dinky's eyes it made him seem vulnerable and, well - human. Perhaps Spike was not that tough after all.

"If I had the chance to become human, I don't know if I'd take it," Spike continued. "But I've heard some scary stories about dogs who did."

This surprised Dinky. "There's other dogs?"

Spike was watching Penny, chatting away with all the dog-prisoners. Dinky turned to look at Penny as well, and when Penny saw him she smiled. This was a different sort of smile than the one she shared with all the others. A little embarrassed now, Dinky smiled back. Spike took it all in.

"We're all in love with Penny in our own way," Spike said. "Even tough guys, like me."

Spike looked around at their surroundings. The high stone walls towered above them, and the guards in the towers were like birds high up in the blue sky.

"I've been in and out of joints like this all my life," he said. "Busted outta every last one of 'em, too. At North Bend, we took fifteen dogs out. Penny's mom dug the tunnel. Great lady. Last place we were together was up at Kingston. I wanted her to bust out with me there, but she said no. She knew her time was up."

Spike then inched closer to Dinky and lowered his voice.

"Penny's mother took the Big Ride at Kingston and never complained. Something happened to her the night Penny was born. She was different after that. She wasn't scared any more. She'd given up the fight, but she was happy. I asked her what happened on the rooftop, but she wouldn't say."

Spike then took another long look up at the guards in the towers.

"I'm askin' you what Penny's mother asked me the night she took the Big Ride at Kingston. Take care of her. Promise me."

"I promise," said Dinky.

Spike nodded. "Good." He then studied Penny as she chatted with the other dogs. "We heard a lot about ya before you came to The Walls. We heard you're the only two-legged dog we can trust."

****

The prison dining hall was a huge, high room with two long tables. The dog-prisoners were all lined up for their lunch ration, each holding an empty bowl in their mouths. There was a steaming pot of slop on the floor at the front of the hall between the two tables. A guard sat on a stool beside the pot, dishing out each portion into the dog-bowls with a long, curved spoon.

Dinky sat between Penny and Spike. All of the dogs were sitting upright like humans, but eating their slop out of the bowls like dogs. Dinky had lowered his face towards the greenish muck and he was just about to start lapping it up with his tongue when he glanced over and saw that Spike was not eating. He was staring into his bowl, contemplating the infinite. One of the prison guards passed by and gave Spike a sharp poke in the ribs with his nightstick.

"Better eat your din-din here, hard ass," the guard laughed. "Road-kill don't grow on trees, ya know!"

When the guard had gone, Spike turned to Dinky.

"I'm bustin' outta here tonight," he whispered. "We're all puttin' on a little show for the warden's birthday. I wasn't sure how I was gonna pull this one off, but you'll be perfect. Now listen..."

****

The theatre at Dog-Alcatraz was not the sort of thing you would see on Broadway, but it had enough seats for the prison staff and the stage was large enough for a professional-type show. There was even a little orchestra pit for a few musicians.

This night, everyone on the staff from the warden down to the janitor had assembled for Warden Smith's birthday celebration. Warden Smith was a sour looking man who rarely smiled. He sat front and center in the first row, flanked by Dr. Pettkus on one side of him and the deputy warden on the other.

A small group of dog-prisoners were holding their instruments in the orchestra pit. At the first signal from the dog-conductor, they started playing some light music and the curtain slowly began to rise. Behind the curtain, a group of dog-prisoners were lined up in a row from one side of the stage to the other. When the curtain got high enough, they all walked in unison to the edge of the stage under the floodlights until they were close to where Warden Smith was sitting.

"Happy birthday Warden Smith!" they all chanted.

Then, some of the individual members of the chorus line began to speak.

"You may be old..." said Old Sparky.

"You may be sick..." said Penny.

"You may be sad and lonely..." said Spike.

"But your host tonight will make you laugh..." said Nerd Dog.

"So, here's the one and only..." said Penny.

"*Dinky!*" chanted the dogs.

All the dogs then looked to stage left, and Dinky suddenly burst onto the stage wearing a straw boater-type hat and a striped jacket. He carried a long cane, and he pointed the cane in the direction of Warden Smith as he ran to the center of the stage. The dog-orchestra then broke into louder music and Dinky launched into a frantic vaudeville routine.

"*Hello, my name is Dinky...some people call me stinky...*"

"*But listen close to what I say to you...*"

"*I may look like a hu-man...but I am telling you-man...*"

"*I'm a dog, I'm a dog, through and through!*"

The chorus line now joined in the singing.

"*He's a dog...he's a dog...he's a filthy, dirty dog...*"

"*Don't be suckered by that face he shows to you...*"

"*He ain't clean...he ain't neat...he eats garbage off the street...*"

"*He's a dog from any human point of view!*"

Warden Smith and all the other clapped and laughed. Dinky waved his cane and held his straw boater hat high in the air.

"*Oh I walk...yes I talk...and I live just down the block...*"

"*They call me human, folks, but that is so untrue!*"

The chorus now rang out.

"*He's a dog...he's a dog...he's a dirty, rotten dog...*"

"*And he's coming to a theatre near you!*"

Dinky pointed to the chorus line as the dog-orchestra continued to play.

"Take a bow, prisoners!" Dinky said. "Hey, Warden Smith...do you know any of these three time losers? Who is that old geezer at the end of the line?"

Old Sparky took a step forward and read from a piece of paper in his hand.

"Hello, everyone," he said. "My name's Old Sparky."

"People, say hi to Old Sparky," Dinky said to the crowd.

"Hi, old Sparky!" the crowd yelled.

Old Sparky continued. "Dinky, I got here yesterday, but I'm the oldest dog in the joint!"

"Oh?" asked Dinky. "Just how old are you, Old Sparky?"

"Well, I've been around so long I can actually remember a time when Warden Smith *didn't* speak in drooling, incoherent, mumbo-jumbo, like he was running for President!"

The audience laughed and pointed to Warden Smith, who rolled his eyes back in a lame effort to look crazy. Dinky now pointed to Penny.

"And what about you, little lady?" Dinky asked. "Can you say a few words to the birthday boy?"

Penny took a step forward and also read from a piece of paper in her hand.

"Happy birthday, Warden Smith!" said Penny. "My name is Penny!"

"Hi, Penny!" said the crowd in unison.

"Penny, why don't you tell the warden a little bit about yourself?" asked Dinky.

"Okay," responded Penny. "Well, Warden Smith, my favorite things are long walks and sad movies. My least favorite thing is rude people. Oh, and also when I've been here 7 days and your men wanna shoot 2000 volts of electricity right up..."

"Penny!" Dinky and the chorus all shouted at once, pointing at her.

Penny put her paw up to her mouth and looked sheepishly at Warden Smith. He was now crying with laughter

Dinky then held up his cane and pointed it towards Spike.

"Hey, tough guy over there!" Dinky yelled out, "You want to say hello to the warden?"

Spike now took a step forward. Like the others, he read from a piece of paper in his hand.

"Happy Birthday Warden Smith!" Spike said. "My name is Spike!"

"Hi, Spike!" said the crowd in unison.

"Spike, I hear you have a special greeting for someone else in the audience?" asked Dinky.

"Oh, yes!" responded Spike. "It's nice to see the prison psychiatrist here, Dr. Pettkus! Before treatment, I had this paranoid notion that everybody hated me for no reason! Dr. Pettkus taught me that they hate me because I'm a no-good psychopath!"

Everyone in the crowd pointed to Dr. Pettkus and laughed. The humorless doctor managed to pull his lips back in a semblance of a grin, but it was a poor effort.

"They tell me tonight I'm supposed to take the Big Ride," Spike went on. "Sorry for being rude, Warden Smith, but maybe I'll just leave now and hijack the first boat home!"

There was more laughter as Spike walked off the stage, waving to the crowd.

"I don't like the food here anyway!" Spike shouted as he disappeared into the wings.

On cue, the dog-orchestra now played louder and the music filled the theatre. Dinky and the other dogs all broke into song.

"He's a dog...he's a dog...he's a dirty, rotten dog..."

"And he's leaving in the middle of the show..."

"There he goes...do you suppose...he might be thumbing his own nose..."

"At all the morons who just sit and watch him gooooo?"

Backstage, Spike quickly ran out of the theatre through a little side door and found himself alone in the prison corridor. He could hear the sounds of Dinky and the other dogs singing on stage, backed by the booming sounds of the dog-orchestra. No one was around because they were all at the show. His plan had worked perfectly! *Just like that part in the Sound of Music, where that singing family escaped*, he told himself. *I saw that in a movie on TV once.*

As he made his way to the main door, Spike could hear Dinky's voice from the theatre.

"I'm not saying that Warden Smith is overweight," Dinky said, "But last week they found Frank Morris hiding out in one of his stomach folds!"

Spike reached the door. "Suckers!" he muttered to himself.

Then Spike opened the door and ran out. He only had time to take a few steps before he was blinded by a sudden spotlight. He froze in his tracks. As his eyes focused, he saw three guards standing in front of him, all pointing shotguns at his head. Then, his eardrums started to rattle from the deafening sound of the prison sirens wailing high up on the towering stone wall.

One of the guards held up Spike's doggie dish. There was a hidden microphone dangling from the bottom.

"You talk too much, Spike baby!" the guard grinned.

Inside the theatre, the music stopped and the house lights came on. In addition to the sirens blaring away outside, the alarm now started ringing in the corridor. The dogs stood silently as they listened. A full lockdown was only moments away, and everyone knew that tough-guy Spike would soon be taking the Big Ride.

****

Midnight had arrived at Dog-Alcatraz. Rain streamed down

on the prison roof, and lightning illuminated the gloomy cellblock in sudden, rapid bursts. From the cells, the dog-prisoners watched as Spike was led down the main corridor towards the door at the far end. The door had been freshly painted a bright yellow.

Spike was flanked by two mournful looking guards, and followed by a preacher who was muttering something in a voice too low for anyone to hear.

Through it all, Spike was stoic. He stared straight ahead. He would be a tough dog to the end. Each dog bid farewell as Spike walked by their cells.

"Take care, buddy-boy," said one dog. "Never let the screws grind you down!"

"Walk tall, tough monkey," said another. "You're loved in this world, you'll be loved in the next!"

"It's a better world we're all bound for, brother!" said another.

Nerd Dog now pressed his face through his cell bars as Spike passed by. He flashed Spike a huge, happy smile.

"See ya at dinner, Spike!" he yelled.

Spike stopped his slow walk and he gave Nerd Dog a long look.

"I'm ready," Spike finally said.

Spike was then led into the little room along with the guards and the preacher, and the bright yellow door closed quietly once they were all inside.

****

Dinky was watching from his cell. Suddenly, he heard the sound of Penny crying. He turned around and saw Penny huddled in the corner.

"I'm a phony!" cried Penny.

Dinky hustled up to her and knelt down on the stone floor.

"Don't say that about yourself, Penny," he pleaded. "You and Spike, you're the bravest dogs I've ever known! Look at you – you let yourself be put into this awful place..."

"Oh, stop it!" Penny interrupted. "I'm a phony and a liar!"

Penny raised her head and looked up at Dinky. Tears were streaming down her face.

"All those flatfoots from the pound were doing a sweep in the bushes down at the dog park. I saw all my friends with their owners, I wanted to show them all how brave I was. So, I ran outta the bushes and bit one of the goons on the ankle! I didn't let myself get caught, I was running away when they got me!"

Penny was sobbing now, and Dinky did not know what to say. "I didn't ever want to come here! No dog does! 'Cause once a dog like me comes in here, you never come out again! Don't look at me like that. Wake up and come to your senses. That's what they all want you to do!"

"Penny..." Dinky stammered, "You're gonna get a home and a family..."

"I said *stop* it!" Penny cried. "You sound just like my

mother and her stupid stories! I'm an ugly dog! I'm an ugly, stupid dog and I'll be put to sleep!"

Penny buried her face in her paws and sobbed. Dinky then heard a guard's voice.

"Hey, Dinky," said the guard. "Got a little something for you!"

Dinky walked up to the guard who stood on the other side of the bars. The guard handed him an envelope. "For you. He wanted me to give you a singing telegram, but I told him, I just don't have the spark for it! Ha! Ha! Ha!"

As the guard laughed, there was a sudden power surge and all the lights in the prison went dim. Dinky opened the envelope and Spike's gold Latin name tag slid out into his hand. The guard walked away, still snickering to himself. Dinky could still hear Penny sobbing behind him. He stared at the shining gold letters, a final gift from a brave friend. Spike was gone, and there was nothing he could do about it.

But there was something he knew he could do. He shouted to the guard.

"Guard! *Hey, you flatfoot!* Get me Dr. Pettkus! I have a confession to make!"

* * * * * * * * * * *

By the time Dr. Pettkus stepped off the boat at Dog-Alcatraz in the wee hours that morning, the storm had subsided a little. There was still the occasional flash of lightning, followed by the ever-present distant boom of thunder. One such lightning flash lit up the entire outside walkway as Dr. Pettkus made his solitary journey up to the prison walls. If anyone had been studying him at that moment, they would have seen a face in torment. His eyes were wild, and his grotesque dog-face was looking even less human than before.

When Dr. Pettkus reached Dinky's cell, Dinky was there to greet him.

"I'm cured!" Dinky announced.

"I don't believe you," Dr. Pettkus snorted.

"It's true, Dr. Pettkus! I lay awake last night just staring into the darkness, and all of a sudden there was a bright light and I heard a voice. It was a voice of prophecy, a voice of illumination. I'm a person, a human being. I don't belong here at all!"

Dr. Pettkus was still skeptical. "Yes, yes, I've heard that all before from other patients."

"I tell you, I'm cured!" Dinky insisted. He waved his hand at the other cells. "They're all just ..."

"What are they, Danky?"

"Why...they're all just stinky dogs!"

A dog-voice now rang out from the corridor. "Hey! I'll have you know I showered today!"

Then there was another dog-voice in response. "Your own pee doesn't count!"

There was the sound of the bark-laugh from all the prisoners. Dr. Pettkus looked around, as if he could sense the sound but not quite hear it.

"Dr. Pettkus, I wasn't a believer at first but your treatment really works. I'm not a dog. I never *was* a dog!"

Dr. Pettkus was still not convinced. "What was the dog looking for in his car, Danky?"

"What kind of dumb question is that?" asked Dinky. "Dogs don't drive!"

"Look into my eyes!" Dr. Pettkus demanded. "What do you see?"

Dinky had to force himself to stare at the alien face that was now extended towards him on the vulture-neck.

"Why, I see..."

"Yes, yes?"

"I see human kindness, and love, and compassion."

"Don't be a fool! What do you see when you look into my eyes? What?"

"I see..."

"Tell me!"

Dinky could not contain himself any longer.

"I see the most despicable human being on the face of the earth!" he shouted. "You are a *madman!*"

Frustrated with himself, Dinky moved away from the cell bars and slumped down on his bunk. He had let Dr. Pettkus get the better of him, and there would never be any early release from Dog-Alcatraz. But Dr. Pettkus was elated. He stepped back from Dinky's cell, his huge red face now beaming with excitement.

"It's a miracle!" Dr. Pettkus shouted, his voice bouncing off the stone walls of the corridor. "Guard! Release this man. He's cured!"

****

It had all happened so quickly. Later that morning, Dr. Pettkus arrived at Dinky's cell with his release papers, freshly signed by Judge Levitts. Dinky was ready for him. He had washed and combed his hair, and he had his bedroll under his arm.

"You will have your competency hearing in three days, Danky," Dr. Pettkus said proudly. "And I know you will pass with flying colors! In the meantime, you are a free man...thanks to no one else but me!"

Dr. Pettkus then led Dinky down the corridor to the guard at the main door. Off to one side of the door was a small control station that contained all the gadgets and switches for the prison's entire electrical system. As they approached the guard, Rex appeared from the control station and bounded up to Dinky. He leaped up and put his paws on Dinky's chest.

"Filthy beast!" muttered Dr. Pettkus. He kept walking, and this now put Dinky slightly behind him with Rex in the middle.

"We don't have much time, so listen good!" Rex said. He then jumped down and trotted beside Dinky. "I'm gonna create a little diversion. When I do, you run into that control room and you flick the last two switches, second row, far right – then first row, second switch, left. Got it?"

"Rex, I don't..."

"Say it! Last two switches, second row..."

"Last two, second row. Rex, I'm confused!"

Rex had no more time for idle chit-chat. He ran up and bit Dr. Pettkus on his arm and started to pull him back towards the cell block.

"You beast! You beast!" Dr. Pettkus screamed. "Mad dog!"

But Rex would not let go. He kept dragging Dr. Pettkus further and further back, away from the main door, and away from Dinky and the control room. The guard at the door ran after Rex, and Dinky was able to slip into the little room without being seen. He tried to remember the instructions that Rex had given him.

"Second row, second row, last switch...I don't know!" Dinky muttered to himself, flicking the switches as best as he could remember.

Rex had been right, and Dinky did not have much time. Through the window of the control room he saw Rex release his bite on Dr. Pettkus and everyone now starting coming back towards the main door. Dinky flicked a couple more switches, then popped out of the room just as the group reached him. Dr. Pettkus was trembling, and the other guards were trying to calm Rex, who kept leaping at Dr. Pettkus in an attempt to bite him again.

"Get that dirty beast away from me!" Dr. Pettkus screamed.

In all the excitement, no one had noticed Dinky in the control room. Rex glanced at him, winked his eye, then calmed down and started to wag his tail. The guard opened the door, and Dr. Pettkus led Dinky out of the cell block.

"Savage dog!" Dr. Pettkus mumbled as they walked along.

Dinky didn't say anything. He was still guarding the bedroll that he held tightly under his arm. Prison security was pretty slack when it came to smuggling contraband in and out of Dog-Alcatraz. If any of the guards had bothered to look close enough, they would have easily seen Penny's frightened little face buried way down in the blankets.

Chapter 7
(The Fugitive)

As soon as the prison boat landed on the shore, Dinky was immediately taken back to the courthouse to appear before Judge Levitts once again. But this hearing lasted all of half a minute. Dinky stood before Judge Levitts with the bedroll still tucked securely under his arm. Judge Levitts shuffled through a stack of papers, then looked impassively at Dinky.

"The accused is released on bail. There will be a final hearing on his mental state in three days. Next case!"

That was it. Dinky was not too sure where to go for the next three days, but his first concern was the little package under his arm and the contents that had to be taken to safety as soon as possible.

Dinky walked out of the courthouse and saw Clyde Daniels waiting for him at the top of the marble steps. He was alone.

"Son," said Clyde, with his calming smile, "Do you think we could have a couple of words somewhere?"

****

Cleaning day at Dog-Alcatraz was never a very long procedure. The cleaning man would sweep the hay out of the cells with a couple of quick strokes of his broom, and then he'd swab the stone floors with a dirty mop. Sometimes fresh hay was put on the floor, and sometimes the old hay just got swept back into the cell again.

On this day, Sam the cleaning man opened the door to Penny's cell and began to push the hay out into the corridor. Sam was a grizzled and toothless old geezer, and legend had it that he had been cleaning out the cells at Dog-Alcatraz since the prison doors first opened in 1939.

Sam knew that Dinky had left the premises, and as he swept the hay he looked around for Penny. He then noticed something sticking out from underneath a few newspapers that had been scattered on the bottom bunk. It looked like the top of Penny's head, with the familiar diamond pattern of white fur.

"Wake up, you little sweetie!" he said. "You are one day later and one day closer. Ha!"

Sam then pushed away the newspapers away with a sweep of his hand. There was no Penny on the bunk, just a crude paper mache dog-head with a big, fake smile.

Sam ran out of the cell. *"Prison break! Prison break!"* he screamed, running towards the guard at the control booth.

Sam had only taken about six steps, when the alarm sounded and the doors to all the cells swung open. Immediately, every dog in the joint came tearing out of their cells and started to charge full-tilt towards the main door at the end of the cell block.

Sam was knocked to the floor by the flood of running dogs.

He tried to get up, but was soon knocked down again by the tide of dogs, large and small. Within seconds there were dogs everywhere.

Dogs were tumbling down the second tier staircase, dogs were skidding on the slippery stone floors, dogs were running down the guards whenever they appeared. The guard at the door stood up in an effort to block the flood of dogs that was rushing towards him, but as soon as he moved, Rex got in tight behind him and pushed him down flat on his face.

It was then a simple matter for Rex to pull the door open with his paw, and the fugitive dogs started pouring through the open door towards the courtyard outside, and freedom.

The dogs ran through the open corridor, then they tore across the cement courtyard and under the big stone archway. It was then a short trip down a gentle embankment to the water. There was no hesitation, no checking the escape plans. As the sirens blared away from the speakers up high on the prison walls, every dog plunged head-first into the water and they all began to swim furiously towards the shore.

Nerd Dog was the last to run out of the prison. He tumbled down the slope to the water and looked around, wide-eyed, and in a panic.

"Hey! Where do I go? What do I do? What do I say?" he stammered.

No one answered, so Nerd Dog closed his eyes and leapt into the water.

There was a street that bordered the harbor, and several cars had stopped at the sound of the sirens coming from the island dog-prison. People got out of their cars and cheered the dogs as they made their bid for freedom. Everyone watched in astonishment as the dogs paddled in a perfect "V" formation, with Old Sparky leading the way.

More cars stopped, and soon a big crowd of people stood on the shore, cheering for the approaching dogs. All the while, the distant sirens blared away from the now-empty prison.

Elvis Dog watched from his position on the sidewalk just above the shore. Another dog had taken a position directly across the street from him. As the fugitive dogs neared the end of their swim, Elvis Dog whistled to the other dog and they both started to cross the street towards each other. This had the effect of stopping traffic in both directions on the busy street, and it created a clear passageway from the shoreline right across to the town square on the opposite side.

When Elvis Dog and the other dog reached the center of each lane of traffic, they flopped over and lay still. None of the stopped cars could now move without running them over. Frustrated motorists honked their horns and yelled, but both dogs continued to lie perfectly still.

One lady motorist ran out of her car and rushed up to Elvis Dog.

"The poor thing has had a heart attack!" she shouted.

"This one, too!" another yelled.

Old Sparky and the other dogs had now reached the shore. They all shook off the cold water and then ran up the slope towards the street. Elvis Dog and the other dog continued to lie motionless, and the stream of fugitive dogs wasted little time in running through the passageway and then into the nearby town square.

When the last dog had run across the street, Elvis Dog and the other dog began to slowly stand up on all fours again. The other dog took off running, but Elvis Dog was lapping up the attention he was getting from the concerned motorist. As he got to his feet, the lady leaned over and stroked his head.

"Your poor dear!" she said. "What's your name?"

Elvis Dog summoned up his best Memphis drawl. "The King!" he answered proudly.

The lady recoiled in shock. Elvis Dog then shot across the street and disappeared into the town square with all the other desperados from the dog-world.

****

Dinky walked down the courthouse steps with Clyde Daniels. They continued a short distance to the town square. Clyde motioned for Dinky to have a seat on one of the benches that surrounded the square.

"I think you know why I'm here," Clyde said, taking a seat. "I just want to ask you one last time. Did you take my daughter's little dog?"

Dinky shook his head. "Mr. Daniels, you came to visit me that night in jail. They told me it was you who left these clothes for me. The lawyer said you arranged things so I wouldn't have to put up any bail money. I know your daughter is still crying over that dog and you should hate me for it..."

"I don't hate you, son," Clyde said softly.

"Mr. Daniels, you lost control in your own home a long time ago," Dinky said. "I know it. I've seen it every day. It eats away at you. I see in your face when you think the rest of the family isn't watching. Mrs. Daniels tells you all the time that you're not the man she married. I hear it day in and day out. Stand up to her. She's wrong!"

Clyde was not about to accept what he was hearing. He moved to stand up, but Dinky held his arm.

"And she's waiting for you to prove her wrong," Dinky said. "It's what she wants! Mr. Daniels, I know this is going to sound crazy to you, but it's like I've lived my whole life over the past few days. It's like...well, it's like I've been born, and I've grown old.

Your daughter will have her dog back, and you'll know it's me! She's a good kid – okay, okay, she's an insufferable brat! There, I said it! But, she's yours and you can't dump her at the roadside. No more dressing up, no more ugly mutt contests. Please!"

Clyde was beginning to understand.

"You have my word," he said calmly.

Clyde moved to stand up again, and Dinky again took his arm. "One more thing..." Dinky now held out the bedroll and carefully pulled back the blankets to reveal Penny huddled inside. "I used to complain about everything, the loneliness of it all. But I didn't know how good I had it. Give Penny a home. I understand now why all this has been happening to me. Take care of her until I can come back!"

Clyde looked at Penny. She was trembling, and she retreated deeper into her hiding place. There was no stopping Clyde this time.

"I'm late," he said. Then he got up and hurried away.

Dinky moved to follow him, but Penny popped out of the blanket and jumped onto the ground.

"Don't," said Penny. "Leave him alone. I know where we can hide! Follow me."

Penny ran across the town square and Dinky hustled behind her to keep up. As they ran, Dinky saw two of the Happy Valley dog pound vans racing down the street with a pack of dogs running ahead of them. Other dogs were now streaming into the town square, where they scattered in all directions.

Dinky had no idea where he was going. He kept his head down and ran after Penny as she shot along like a little bullet, leading him in a crazy zig-zag pattern through the busy streets and sidewalks of the city.

****

The Happy Valley Feed and Tack warehouse had been long abandoned. Penny had always made it her home, but it was a lonely place. It was one of those condemned buildings on the outskirts of town that was always going to be turned into a shopping center, or a community swimming pool, or something that the general public would enjoy. But nothing like that ever happened. The old building was still an eyesore fifty years after the last Happy Valley kid had thrown the last rock through the last glass window.

Old Sparky and the other fugitive dogs were hiding out on the main floor. They lounged around in the midst of all the dust covered boxes and broken glass and all the cobwebs. They caught a quick snooze where they could find a comfortable spot, and they ate whatever scraps were being passed around. Life on the run was no picnic, but it beat Dog-Alcatraz – especially after a seven day visit.

Penny always loved the warehouse rooftop. Her mother had told her that she had been born on the rooftop with all her brothers, and it was her favorite spot. Now, she was sharing her special spot with Dinky. They had a view of the whole city and they sat for a long time in silence, watching the lights of the Happy Valley County Fair in the distance.

"I was at that fair," Dinky said. "Seems like a hundred years ago."

There was a long silence, then Penny spoke. "I was born in this building. Right here, actually. My mother wanted a quiet place. She told me she barely made it up the stairs when her babies started coming. She had ten of us that night. Me and my nine brothers. There was nobody to help her, not like with most dogs. She was all alone."

"I have a vague memory of my mother before I got adopted out," Dinky said. "And word has it that dear old dad took one look at his ugly son and was never seen again. Not by us, anyway."

"I was the last one born," Penny continued. "The runt of the litter. You ever heard that term?"

"I've heard it," Dinky said, staring ahead.

"My mother told me she almost died when it came to me. Then, after nine boys, when she saw she had a daughter, well she thought that maybe all the effort was worth it after all. I was so tiny she didn't think I'd live through the night. But she held me close and I pulled through. My brothers had just been born, but they knew enough not to interfere. I had my mother all to myself that night. It was the one and only time in my life."

"Spike told me something happened to your mother that night," said Dinky.

"She had ten children all by herself, that's what happened," said Penny, smiling. "My brothers just drifted away. They're all gone now."

Dinky was still looking straight ahead and Penny realized that he had forgotten that a little dog was speaking to him.

"Hey! Down here!" Penny laughed. "I'm a dog, remember?" Dinky looked down, then took Penny into his arms.

"I want you to take me somewhere tomorrow, Dinky." Penny said. "I want more than anything else in this world for my friends to see me like they have never seen me before."

****

The George Hume Memorial Dog Park was about block from the Happy Valley town square. The place was always full of dogs of all shapes and sizes. Dinky had been there countless times before, but he had never had to lead another dog on a leash through the maze of dog trails and criss-crossing pathways. And doing this on two new human legs did not make things any easier for him.

Penny was beside herself with joy. She was running ahead at full steam, with her nose tilted proudly in the air. She pulled so hard on her leash that Dinky stumbled to keep up. She was greeting every dog she saw as they passed by: *"Hello there! How ya doing! Beautiful day for a walk!"*

"This is the happiest day of my life!" she exclaimed, as Dinky led her along. "I have an owner and I'm respectable! Oh, I can't wait for my best friends to see me now."

Penny then spotted her best friends.

"There they are!" she shouted. "Hey, hey, hey! Pals, it's me! Sadie! Sam! It's me, Penny!"

Penny now strained at the leash and Dinky broke into a run as they crossed the lawn.

"Sadie! Sam!" Penny shouted again. "It's me!"

They finally reached the two dogs and their owners. The dogs stared at Penny, then looked curiously at each other as if they were not sure what to say to her. One of their owners smiled at Dinky.

"Hello, there," the owner said. "First visit to the dog park?"

Dinky shook his head. "Well, to tell you the truth, not exactly," he replied.

The other two dogs backed away a little, and Dinky let go of the leash as Penny ran up to them.

"Pals," said Penny, "It's me. Don't you recognize me?"

The dogs looked at each other again. Then Sadie turned to Penny.

"Why, you're that ugly little dog who's always hiding in the bushes!" Sadie exclaimed.

Penny was shattered. "I'm Penny," she said quietly. "Don't you know me?"

The two dogs didn't respond. Sam broke into a muffled laugh, and Sadie lowered her eyes and stared vacantly at the ground. There was a long pause. Then their owners gave them both a tug on the leash, and they all walked away, dogs and owners, without saying anything more.   As Penny watched them go, the two dogs did not bother to look back at her.

Dinky had witnessed all of this, and his heart was breaking for Penny. Still, she didn't complain. She watched, expressionless, as the two dogs walked away, but when she looked up at Dinky again she had found her usual happy grin.

"Come on," she said. "I'll show you where the food is!" Penny lead Dinky to the far end of the dog park, then down a short flight of stairs to a fenced area with a row of dumpsters lining the fence. Dinky hesitated before they got any further.

"Penny, are you sure about this?" he asked.

"Hey, don't be such a snob!" Penny said. "We always wondered what the pickings would be like during the day, but none of us stray dogs ever had the nerve to get this far."

Penny had no sooner got her words out when two huge stray dogs came out from behind one of the dumpsters and snarled at them. Dinky and Penny stopped. The two dogs crept closer and growled.

"You get outta here!" one of them said, baring his teeth.

A homeless man popped his head out of the dumpster and threw a bottle in the direction of the two dogs. It sailed past them and shattered on the pavement. The dogs hesitated, then turned and ran away.

"Thanks," said Dinky to the homeless man. The man didn't say anything back. He popped his head down into the dumpster again and the dumpster lid closed on top of him with a loud bang. Dinky and Penny walked around the dumpster, then turned the corner.

There were homeless people everywhere. Some were pushing shopping buggies that contained all their possessions. Others scrambled for something in the other dumpsters. A few of them were sleeping under makeshift cardboard shelters. These were the people for whom life was a day to day struggle to survive.

Dinky watched, and he saw himself.

After a very long walk, Dinky and Penny finally thought they might find something to eat in a pile of boxes they found on a loading dock behind a large supermarket. As they picked through the rotten tomatoes and the throwaway scraps of meat, a young grocery clerk in a green apron came out onto the dock with a box of lettuce scraps from the produce department. He looked at the sad pair, the destitute man and his scruffy little dog. Dinky and Penny were about to run off, when the clerk tossed the box towards them.

"Here" he said, "Help yourself."

The clerk went back inside, and Dinky tore off the top of the box and started to rummage through the lettuce. They had found a newspaper in the pile of boxes, and Dinky started to wrap the better pieces of lettuce in the newspaper. He looked over at Penny and gave her one of the choice lettuce leaves.

"Hey, thanks Dinky," Penny said happily.

Dinky watched Penny as she gulped down the lettuce.

"Penny, you're starving!"

"I'm always hungry," Penny said, as she stuffed another piece of lettuce into her mouth.

Dinky picked Penny up and held her close.

"I love you, Penny," he said. "We're both gonna find a home, you'll see."

Penny finished gulping down the lettuce snack and Dinky put her gently down on the loading dock. As he did this, some of the lettuce spilled out of the newspaper and Dinky bent down to pick up the scraps.

"Dinky, would you love me better if I was one of those show dogs you could take home to your family?" Penny asked.

"Well, if I had two wishes, that one would be my second wish."

"Dinky!" Penny now sounded concerned.

"No, I would *not* love you better if you were a show dog!"

"Dinky, look," said Penny.

Penny pointed to the headline in the newspaper. It read:

'POLICE CLOSE IN ON FUGITIVE DOGS'

Dinky quickly picked up the lettuce scraps and wrapped them up in the newspaper.

"Let's get outta here," he said.

****

Two days had now passed, and Dinky was going stir-crazy. In the abandoned warehouse that night, all the fugitive dogs were gathered together on the main floor. Penny was talking with the little dog that had asked Dinky to keep an eye out for her that night in the alley. Dinky sat in the middle of the group, eating the remains of someone's fast-food meal. He took a half-bite, then lay the food down beside him.

"This used to taste so wonderful when I got it out of our own garbage back home," he said.

"Yeah," said Nerd Dog. "There's nothing like home cooking!"

The other dogs reacted with their bark-laugh at this remark. Old Sparky then wandered in and joined the group.

"Brothers," he began. Then he looked at Penny. "And sister...we took this stranger in because Rex vouched for him the other night in the alley. And we're all big brothers to Penny. Now, she's a wanted dog along with most of you here. And if we don't watch our backsides, we all headed back to prison for the Big Ride."

The dogs all now looked at Dinky.

"Dogs that run away from the pound are not exactly priority #1 with the police. But a serial dognapper! Now, we owe our brother Dinky here a big debt of gratitude for helping us make our break outta that awful place..."

"Hear, hear!" Nerd Dog shouted. The others stared at him.

Old Sparky then turned to Dinky. "You keep talking about this mysterious wish you get in a couple of days," he said. The wish that you say is gonna turn you back into a dog again. If you really believe in that wish like you say you do..."

"I do believe it," insisted Dinky.

"Fine. Then turn yourself in."

The other dogs gasped at this remark. Penny trotted up to Old Sparky.

"Sparky, don't," she said.

"Won't matter where you are when you make your wish, will it?" Old Sparky asked. "It's *you* they want. And we'll all be a little safer."

"He can't go back," said Penny. "Don't make him do it!"

"You gotta go to that hearing, Dinky." Old Sparky then turned to the group. "We found out that Mr. Daniels put up Dinky's bail. If he doesn't go to that hearing, Mr. Daniels loses his house. You know that already, don't you Dinky?"

"I know it," said Dinky quietly.

Old Sparky looked thoughtfully around the huge, dusty room. It was dark outside, but a little light came into the old building from the streetlights nearby.

"Dinky, when I was a young buck Hume Park was a lot more fun than it is today," Old Sparky said. "A lot of the old dogs hung out down by the wishing well. I used to sit with 'em, hear 'em tell all their stories, listen to their jokes. They used to say that no matter how bad things got for a dog, there'd always be one friend left to help out. I used to laugh at those silly old dogs. Now, I'm an old dog."

Old Sparky had finished. He looked at Dinky and lay his head gently down on the floor. Dinky knew where he had to go.

****

Dinky was saying his good-byes at the big warehouse door. He lifted Penny up and gave her a big kiss on the cheek.

"A couple of days from now, I'm gonna come looking for you," he said.

"Ohhhhhhhhh!" all the dogs said.

"I love all of you, too!" Dinky said.

Nerd Dog now ran up to Dinky, sobbing uncontrollably. He gave Dinky a warm embrace.

"Buddy," he sobbed, tears running down his cheeks, "Be careful!"

"And you be strong," Dinky said. "Remember Spike."

Nerd Dog now pointed to the sky. "Now there was a *dog*!" he exclaimed.

Dinky was just about to leave the dogs when the clouds parted and more moonlight streamed down on the warehouse. From the corner of his eye, Dinky thought he caught a glimpse of something shining near the edge of the building. Slowly, he turned his head towards the front wall of the warehouse. He was right. There, just peeking out from behind the old bricks at the far end of the wall, Dinky spotted the freshly-polished toe of a military boot. Trouble was - literally - right around the corner. He turned back to the dogs who were all crowded around the front door.

Penny knew that worried look. "Dinky, what's wrong?" she asked.

"Run!" screamed Dinky.

As soon as he shouted, a huge roar sounded above the warehouse rooftop and a military helicopter came into view. The helicopter was flying low, and it had its searchlight beams sweeping back and forth over the ground. A team of armed SWAT police ran around from the side of the building and headed towards the warehouse entrance.

The dogs scattered, and Dinky started to run in the direction of a vacant lot next door. There was shouting and the occasional shot from a military rifle being fired into the air. The helicopter roared past the warehouse, then it made an abrupt turn and headed back again, engines wailing, hovering overhead now with the powerful searchlight beams streaming down and lighting up the whole area like it was high noon.

Dinky didn't get very far. The SWAT team was on him in an instant, and he was dragged back to the warehouse. When he reached the door, a police car came screeching up directly in front of him. Rex bounded out of the police car along with two police officers. The SWAT team pushed Dinky towards the police officers and then ran back into the warehouse to flush out more of the fugitive dogs.

"He's all yours!" one of them shouted.

Rex watched Dinky as the two policemen pushed him into the back seat of the police car.

"You never listen, do you?" asked Rex, casually as always.

"Come on, Rex," one of policemen said.

Rex took his place in the very back of the car behind the metal grate. As the police drove away, Rex put his nose up to the grate to get as close as he could to Dinky.

"I'm sorry, Dinky," Rex said. "I thought if all the other dogs ran away from that dreadful place instead of just you and Penny, it would take the heat off the two of you. I screwed up big time."

Dinky reached around and gave Rex a fake punch on the jaw through the grate. Rex managed a smile.

"Where will Penny go now?" Dinky wondered aloud.

"Don't you understand, Dinky?" said Rex. "Dogs like that just hide out their whole life. Where is she now? What difference does it make? She's in another rotting old building that's gonna come crashing down on her head! She's hiding under somebody's porch until she gets a warm welcome with a load of buckshot! Dinky..."

Rex now lowered his voice and Dinky inched closer to him.

"You have a home to go back to and so do I," Rex said. "Don't be a fool!"

"Rex, how the heck did the riot cops know where we were?"

"Are you kidding me? You didn't see it when you looked into the eyes of that quack doctor? He asked you to look into his eyes, didn't he? You know why? *I know why!*"

One of the policemen in the front seat now turned back and faced Dinky.

"You talkin' to yourself back there, doggie-man?"

Dinky said nothing, and Rex moved away from the grate. They all rode the rest of the way in silence.

Dinky didn't know this, but at that moment Penny was huddled alone under a parked trailer rig as she watched the police car take Dinky back to the station. This was not exactly an old building, or someone's back porch, but in the end Rex had it nailed. It didn't matter. She had no place else to go.

****

Outside the police station a large crowd had gathered to catch a glimpse of the serial dognapper whose name had made the headlines for the last few days. Dr. Pettkus stood on the top step of the police station, shouting to anyone who would listen.

"This man was not cured!" he yelled. "He fooled me! He fooled you! He will be sent back to the pound to face execution!"

The police led Dinky through the crowd, gently pushing people out of the way as they went along. As usual, Rex followed obediently behind. At the edge of the crowd, young Henry Beamish was watching with his mother. Suddenly, Henry broke away from his mother's hand and scampered through the police guard and ran right up to Dinky. He pointed an accusing finger at Dinky and stomped his foot.

"I know you!" Henry shouted defiantly. "You're the man who eats dogs!"

Dinky looked at Henry and made a loud barking noise, as if he was about to swallow him in one gulp. This caused the boy genius to spin around and leap screaming into the arms of his mother.

"Mommy! Mommy!" young Henry wailed.

The crowd was appalled at Dinky's behavior.

"A monster!" someone yelled.

"Awful!" said another.

"He eats dogs!" gasped someone else.

****

Also watching from a safe distance in the nearby alley was Old Sparky and some of his stray-dog pals. "If the good doctor wants dogs, we'll give him dogs," Old Sparky said. "You all know what to do."

Chapter 8
(Doggie Daddy)

Dinky's competency hearing was the hottest ticket in town. People had lined up for hours in order to get a seat in the gallery. The courtroom was packed, and a large crowd stirred around outside. Some people gave interviews to the television crews that had set up tents in the town square. Others lingered on the courthouse steps, hoping to get a glimpse of a witness, or be the first to catch a bit of news from inside.

In the courtroom, Dinky sat at a table next to his court-appointed lawyer. The county prosecutor was questioning Sam the cleaning man from the dog prison. Clearly out of his element, Sam shifted back and forth in his seat and tugged nervously at his new necktie.

"And what did Dr. Pettkus do when the accused called him a madman?" the prosecutor asked.

"He just got all happy-like, and he started in a yipin' that the Dinky man was cured."

"And then?"

"Well, later I went to that darned cage and the other one wasn't there. That's all I know."

"No more questions!"

Dinky's lawyer then stood up and faced Sam the cleaning man.

"Sir, did you actually see Mr. Dinky take the dog Penny out of the cell?" he asked.

"Nope, but I know he done it."

"Well sir, if you didn't see him do it, then you don't know for sure that he did it, now do you?"

"Yep, I know for sure."

"*How* do you know?"

"I heard 'em all talking."

"You heard talking?"

"I said I heard talking. You hard-a hearing there?"

"You heard *who* talking, sir?"

"The *dogs*, you stupid fool!"

****

Dinky's lawyer was now questioning the leader of the SWAT team that had conducted the raid.

"Tell me, sir," said the lawyer, "Of all the places to conduct your raid, why did you go to the old Feed and Tack warehouse on Water Street? Why that location as opposed to any other?"

"It was Dr. Pettkus who told us to go there," came the response.

This brought a gasp from the gallery.

"Oh, Dr. Pettkus! And what did Dr. Pettkus tell you?"

"He said he knew we should look in the old warehouse, because..."

"Go on!"

"Well, because he smelled 'em all in the air."

"I see! He sniffed the air, did he?"

The prosecutor jumped up. "The witness used the word smelled, not sniffed."

"He sniffed! Just like a low-down sniffing..."

"Objection!"

****

Dr. Pettkus was now on the stand being questioned by Dinky's lawyer. He was clearly a tormented soul. His Alsatian Wolfhound features were even more doglike now, and his entire persona suggested a man in the midst of a bizarre and painful transformation.

"I did not sniff the air!" he shrieked. "I took the air! Dogs sniff. Humans take. If you were human, counselor, you'd know the difference!"

"Strike that remark!" said the lawyer.

"What is orange and red and looks good on a lawyer? Fire!"

Everyone laughed. Even the stone-faced Judge Levitts could not suppress a slight smile. Now thrilled with his new popularity, Dr. Pettkus stood up and faced the gallery.

"What do you call a lawyer with an I.Q. of 50? Your Honor! Ha! Ha!"

Dr. Pettkus stopped laughing and looked up at Judge Levitts who was now scowling down at him from his perch on the bench. He broke into an embarrassed grin, and his enormous dog-smile made everyone gasp. Then, he slowly extended his left foot, took off his shoe and sock, and began to scratch his left cheek with his long dog-toes. In this impossibly contorted position, he let out a squealing, high-pitched fart.

"What was that noise?" Judge Levitts demanded.

"It was nothing, Master!"

"I heard a noise."

"I broke wind! I'm sorry."

Dr. Pettkus then broke into another grin. For the first time, he was now aware of the beginnings of sharp dog-teeth and a mouth and jaw three times too big for a normal human face. Terrified, he slapped his hand over his face. Then, he barked.

"There's that sound again," yelled Judge Levitts.

"Sorry-sorry-sorry!" pleaded Dr. Pettkus, as he slapped his mouth with his other hand, almost knocking himself over.

"Do something!" Judge Levitts ordered. "Clench your buttocks, man!"

Dr. Pettkus tried to control himself but it was a hopeless task. He barked again and grinned at Judge Levitts. Helpless and embarrassed, he lowered his head and licked his lips with his long, red tongue. Tears streamed out of his eyes as he tried desperately to control his violently twitching body.

"Did I make a boo-boo, Master?" he asked Judge Levitts.

Dinky's lawyer continued his questioning.

"Sir, you told the court the other day that you attended – what was it? The Blitnik Academy in Budapest?"

"Yes! That is my alma mater, yes!" said Dr. Pettkus proudly.

"The Blitnik Academy...Tell us, are you a real doctor – *doctor*?"

Dr. Pettkus began to stammer.

"The toe bone is connected to the foot bone..."

"That's enough, sir!" Judge Levitts warned.

"And the foot bone is connected to the ankle bone..."

"Sir!" bellowed Judge Levitts.

"What did you study at the Blitnik Academy, doctor?" the lawyer now asked.

Dr. Pettkus took a deep breath and tried his last stab at sanity.

"The brain!"

"That all?"

"The infinite recesses of the human psyche – yes! The complexity of the mind!"

"Did you study – oh, I don't know – how to get a bone by fetching the morning paper? The Happy Valley Gazette perhaps?"

Dr. Pettkus jumped up from the witness box and pointed to the lawyer.

"I hired you to sue that dating service! Where's my money?"

"Strike that!" yelled the lawyer. "It's non-responsive!"

"Stick to the point," Judge Levitts warned him.

"But Judge! Two dates they say! Happy or your money back. First date..."

To make his point, Dr. Pettkus stuck out his first finger. Raving now, contorting and sweating, he failed to notice that his finger was now a long dog-toe.

"First date..." Dr. Pettkus continued. "Now, I myself am no prize! But this girl! Yikie-yee! Hair on only one side of her head, and cross-eyed. I want a little action, you know, and she start to kiss the gearshift of her car!"

There was a silence in the courtroom and Dr. Pettkus felt compelled to explain himself.

"You see Judge, she cross-eyed..."

"We understand!" shouted Judge Levitts. *"Enough!"*

Dr. Pettkus now held up two dog-fingers. "And second date?" Dr. Pettkus now stared at his hand – the long finger-toes, the fur. Reality was starting to sink in.

"Second date – a real – dog!"

"Ah," the lawyer continued. "But there was a time when you were 'catnip' to all the ladies, isn't that true?"

"That's not true," Dr. Pettkus shot back. "I have always been a loser!"

"Oh?" the lawyer said. "Is your son a loser, too?"

"My-my-my-my-my what?" Dr. Pettkus stammered.

"Your ugly son! When you first laid eyes on your ugly son, you recoiled in horror and you abandoned both your child and his mother, did you not?"

Dinky now leaned forward in his seat, sensing that a long hidden secret was about to be revealed.

"The mother was sent to the union workhouse where she died!" the lawyer continued. "Disgraced by a heartless cad! And your own son? That poor, ugly, pathetic runt? He got a ticket to the Happy Valley Dog Pound!"

The gallery was now buzzing with astonished voices.

"The pound? The dog pound?"

The lawyer now pointed at Dr. Pettkus. "Your guilt was like poison in your own soul! And you tried to escape that guilt by making a pact with the devil! You were given a wish, and the wish drove you to madness! But dog or man, sir, your shame rings in your ears to this very day!"

"That is a lie!" Dr. Pettkus stammered. "I am a graduate of the Blitnik Academy!"

Dinky's lawyer now moved over to an easel that had been set up directly in front of the witness box. On the easel were some blown-up photographs covered by a white sheet. The lawyer pulled back the sheet to reveal a color photograph of the Blitnik Academy.

"Do you recognize this building, doctor?" the lawyer asked.

Dr. Pettkus gave a huge, happy grin.

"Yes! Yes! That is the Blitnik Academy, accredited by the University of Budapest. My school!"

"Doctor, I put it to you..." the lawyer went on, "The Blitnik Academy is not in Buda-*pest*. It is located at 310 3rd Avenue, six blocks from this courtroom!"

Everyone now leaned closer to get a good look at the photograph. On the front window of the school there were some painted images of dogs in graduating gowns being handed diplomas.

"The Blitnik Academy is an obedience school for dogs!" the lawyer shouted triumphantly. He then turned to a photograph of an empty classroom.

"That is my classroom!" shouted Dr. Pettkus.

There was another photograph of a group of dogs posing in front of their trainer.

"And those are my friends!"

And another photograph of a group of dogs holding hockey sticks.

"And that is my team!"

Then, a final life-size photograph of an Alsatian Wolfhound.

"And that is my-my-my *mother*!"

Dr. Pettkus then tilted his dog-head to one side as if to listen to something coming from outside.

"I hear them!" he shouted. "Do you hear them? My friends all call to me!"

Outside the courthouse, people stood and watched the scene in front of them in stunned disbelief. Penny and the local dogs had surrounded the courthouse steps, along with hundreds of other dogs from all over the county. All were engaged in one long, loud, dog-howl.

Excited, Dr. Pettkus put his paw to his ear and listened to the chorus of howling canines.

"I'm coming, my dear buddies!" he said. "I'm on my way!"

Dr. Pettkus now let out his own howl, and with this cry his features morphed into the last phase of a completely formed Alsatian dog-head. Now a species unto himself, he leaped out of the witness box and landed on the large dog photograph.

"Mommy!" Dr. Pettkus exclaimed.

The photograph then crashed on top of Dinky, and his own head popped out exactly where the dog head had been. He looked up and saw Dr. Pettkus hovering over him.

"Daddy!" Dinky cried tearfully.

"Sonny!" Dr Pettkus responded.

Dr. Pettkus pulled Dinky towards him and gave him a huge dog-kiss right on his mouth with his slobbering canine lips. Dinky gagged and tried furiously to shake off the photograph.

Outside the courthouse, Penny and the other dogs now swayed in unison and sang the same tune they all sang in the theatre at Dog-Alcatraz.

"He's a dog...he's a dog...Dinky's daddy is a dog..."

"And we only have one thing to say to youuuu..."

"Get a lawyer, go and sue me..."

"But dear daddy, you're a loony..."

"You're a stinky, wormy doggie through and through!"

****

Dinky's lawyer had done his job. As he approached Judge Levitts, the outcome of the hearing was no longer in doubt.

"Your Honor," said the lawyer, "I move that the entire testimony of that last witness be struck from the record! He is no doctor! He is a dog!"

"The People drop the charges, Your Honor," said the prosecutor.

"Case dismissed!" said Judge Levitts, banging his gavel.

Dinky's supporters all cheered. Dinky looked stunned as his lawyer wrapped him in a big bear hug and slapped him on the back.

Dr. Pettkus was now screaming and jumping up and down, demanding that he be let out to run with his doggie-friends. All of the available police and court officials were trying to tackle him, but he kept slipping out of their grasp and running wildly around the courtroom.

Dinky was quickly ushered out of the building. When he got outside, he saw a few hapless dog pound officials trying to chase the stray dogs out of the town square. It was a futile task. Penny and the other dogs would part to make a path for the officers, then rapidly close ranks behind them and run up and nip at their heels. There was an ocean of dogs, wave after wave of them, and the frustrated dog-catchers could do nothing about it.

As Dinky stood and watched, the huge courthouse doors flew open, and the men in the white coats dragged Dr. Pettkus to a waiting police ambulance. He was now wearing a straight-jacket that was tightly belted around his twisting body, and he still yelled out to all of his doggie-friends.

"I'm coming my friends!" he shrieked. "We will all be together! Where's my sonny-boy?"

Dr. Pettkus let out another long howl as the men shoved him into the ambulance. He pushed his grinning dog-head out the window and looked back at Dinky. The ambulance took off with its sirens blaring. Dr. Pettkus then extended one of his huge dog-paws and waved farewell to his only son. His big ears flapped wildly in the wind as the ambulance roared down the street.

"Sonny!" yelled Dr. Pettkus, his voice rapidly fading away. "Daddy loves you-uuuu! I'm so sorry!"

Dinky watched this spectacle from the courthouse steps, and his father's parting words echoed in his ears long after the ambulance had disappeared into traffic. *Daddy loves you! I'm so sorry!* What irony in those two simple phrases! Dinky always yearned for the love of his parents, but in the end it was all drowned in sorrow. Dinky knew he would never lay eyes on his father again.

And like his brief relationship with doggie-daddy, the case of The People versus Dinky had come to an end.

Chapter 9
(Dinky Gets His Wish)

Dinky was now a free man, but he had nowhere to go and not a cent to his name. His lawyer bounded out of the courthouse and ran up beside him.

"Without doubt, you are the most interesting client I have ever had," the lawyer said, slapping Dinky on the back once again.

"Really?" Dinky said, still bewildered by everything that had happened.

The lawyer handed Dinky his business card. "Dinky, you may need this one day," he said. "If you ever fracture your skull and get brain damage, or if you snap your spine and become a ventilator quadriplegic, give me a call. I will personally come to the IC unit to sign you up. I don't send a member of my staff, like a lot of other shysters out there. But of course I have to charge for mileage and parking."

"Gee, thanks," Dinky said, staring at the card.

The lawyer lowered his voice. "To tell you the truth, if you're not injured at all, it really doesn't matter. The lawyers just have to hire the right people, if you know what I mean. Say, you haven't already been in an accident, have you? No bonk on the noggin?"

"I don't think so," said Dinky.

The lawyer shrugged and walked down the steps. Clyde Daniels now passed by, followed by Mary and Daisy.

"What are you going to do now, son?" Clyde asked him.

Dinky's reply was simple. "Go home," he said.

Clyde thought about this, then continued down the stairs. Mary Daniels would still not look at Dinky, but as Daisy passed by him she gave him one of her dirty looks and screwed up her mouth. Dinky just smiled. Others were now pouring out of the courtroom, but no one seemed to pay any attention to Dinky. His moment of fame had come and gone. All of the television news crews had removed their equipment from the town square, and there wasn't a stray dog in sight. It was like none of it had ever been real.

Dinky stuck his hands in his empty pockets and walked over to the town square. He sunk down on one of the park benches and contemplated his next move. He watched people pass by him in the square. Everyone seemed to be happy, and they all looked so busy with a purpose and a destination. Dinky had none of that. He could not wait to use his wish and finally go back to the comforts of his home and family.

Dinky looked up at the clock in the middle of the town square. It was almost four o'clock. A few more hours and it would all be over.

As Dinky sat on the bench, a homeless man walked up to him with a shopping cart full of bottles and empty soda cans. He was leading a dog on a leash that was tied to the shopping cart. The man held out a bottle and gestured for Dinky to take a drink.

"You like a little drinky-poo there, buddy?" the man slurred.

"A drink wouldn't hurt, I guess," Dinky replied, taking the bottle.

"It's after shave," the dog said.

Dinky handed the bottle back without taking a drink. The man shrugged, then took a huge swig himself. He smacked his lips and smiled brightly, then wandered off with the shopping cart and the dog in tow. Then, Dinky heard Penny's voice coming from under the bench.

"A dog's life isn't so bad after all, huh? Some dogs, anyway!"

Dinky looked down and poked his head under the bench.

"Penny!" he exclaimed.

"Shhhhhh," Penny warned. "Those dog catchers from the pound are everywhere! They probably got their eyes on you right now."

Dinky straightened up and looked around. He could not see anyone watching him.

"Word is, they're not gonna keep you locked up any more," Penny whispered.

"Yeah."

"By my reckoning Dinky, you can make your wish tonight!"

Dinky bent down again and looked at Penny. "Where you gonna be at 9:30?"

"I'll be far away from here, Dinky," Penny said. "This is good-bye!"

"No!" shouted Dinky.

"Hush up!" Penny warned him again. "Do you want to get us thrown back into prison?"

"Penny, you can't go!" pleaded Dinky.

But Penny had made up her mind. "Old Sparky and the others, they've decided it's just too risky to stay in the city any longer," she said. "They're all hiding out in Hume Park, waiting for me to join 'em. We're all gonna cross over the big highway and head off into the next county. No more cities, Dinky. And no more running from the pound. It's the only way!"

"Penny, I'm in love with you," Dinky said. "I won't let you go!"

"Dinky, we both better face reality," Penny said. "I'm sure as heck not gonna be welcome in your home! And life with me on the street? Well, you had a taste of that the other day, didn't you? A diet of garbage and you scatter like mice every time a car drives by. No life!"

"I don't care," Dinky insisted.

"You'll care plenty a week from now and by then we'll all be too far away and it'll be too late to go home. I've been a homeless dog my whole life, Dinky. I know!"

129

Penny moved a little closer to Dinky. "Gimme your hand," she said softly. "It'll be okay."

Dinky moved his hand over to the end of the bench, then slipped it down over the edge. Penny nuzzled up to the back of his hand and closed her eyes. She gave Dinky's hand a lick with her little tongue.

"You can't come with me, Dinky," Penny said, her eyes brimming with tears. "And you'll never, ever be able to make it in this world as a person. You know and I know, you only have one choice. You make your wish and you go back home!"

Dinky sat back on the bench. "I can't," he whispered. "I can't live without you, Penny."

Penny slowly inched herself out from her hiding place under the bench. She looked up at Dinky.

"Don't you worry about me," she smiled. "My mother always told me I'd be okay! Me! Her sick little child – the runt of the litter! Something *did* happen the night I was born. My mother knew I'd always be okay! You know how she knew?"

"Penny, don't go," Dinky cried.

"An angel told her!"

"No!" shouted Dinky.

Penny then turned and ran across the town square. Dinky stood up and started to run after her, but he crashed into someone on a bicycle and both fell to the ground. When he picked himself up again, Penny was gone.

"Hey," said the cyclist. "Watch where you're goin', will ya?"

The cyclist picked up his bicycle and went on his way.

Dinky continued to look around the town square, but Penny was nowhere to be seen.

* * * * * * * * * * * *

Penny scurried down the sidewalk. Her eyes darted quickly from side to side, ever watchful of any pound officials who might be lurking in the shadows, ready to pounce. She was so tiny that a lot of people on the sidewalk did not even see her, and she was constantly trying to avoid the steady flow of kids who came streaming by her on bikes and skateboards. She was able to get a couple of blocks from the town square, when suddenly she saw one of the dog pound vans pull up to the street in front of her. Penny made a rapid u-turn and ran back down the sidewalk.

Then, she made a hard left into a back alley that ran to the next cross street further ahead. This alley served as a delivery route for a number of restaurants on the main street, and Penny was brought to a momentary halt by the delicious aroma of the food coming from Fong's, the best Chinese restaurant in town. How hungry she always was! One of the cooks from Fong's was taking a break, and he flicked his cigarette butt at her.

"No food!" he said.

Penny ducked the cigarette and kept running. She was now aware of two other dogs following her down the alley. As she ran,

131

she looked back and saw the two tough dogs she and Dinky had seen that day at the row of dumpsters near the dog park. The dogs broke into a fast run as soon as she looked at them, and Penny knew it was only a matter of time before they caught up with her. Running now with all the strength in her little body, she bolted ahead and reached the end of the alley.

She didn't get very far. Just as she ran out of the alley to the next sidewalk, she looked back at the two dogs and they were almost upon her. But before she could look ahead again, Penny ran headfirst into the dog-catcher's extended boot. *Smack!* The blow knocked her out into the street and Penny squealed loudly as she tumbled on the pavement. She quickly picked herself up again, but her right leg had been injured and she could no longer run. Disoriented now and in pain, she limped around in a circle, having completely lost her sense of direction. It didn't matter. A second later, she was scooped up into the dog-catcher's large net. She was now trapped, and totally helpless.

"Gotcha!" said the dog-catcher with a big grin.

The tough dogs had already rounded the corner, and they had stopped on the sidewalk beside the dog pound van. The dog-catcher tossed each of them a bone.

"Thanks for your help," the dog-catcher said. "Now beat it!"

As the tough dogs took off, the dog-catcher twisted the net a few times, and held it up high. He proudly examined his latest catch. "Time to go back home, girlie!" he said.

Penny was then thrown into the dog pound van with a few of the other dogs that had escaped from Dog-Alcatraz. They rode along in silence.

"Well, we made a good go of it, anyway," one of them said. "We can all be proud."

"I'm sorry, Penny," another dog said. "I guess some things aren't meant to be."

Despite her injured leg, Penny managed to get herself up on a stack of empty dog cages in the back of the van, and she looked out the rear window. As the van pulled away from a stop sign, she saw Dinky cross the street behind them. He walked slowly, awkwardly, with his head down. He bumped into someone and apologized. He then steadied himself and kept walking.

****

The boat ride to Dog-Alcatraz only took a few minutes, and Penny soon found herself being led down the main cell block with the other captured fugitives. The guard at the control room grinned as they all marched by him.

"Welcome back, poochies," he said.

Penny was taken back to her cell. It was now early evening and the sun was going down. She looked up at the tiny, square window at the top of the stone wall. Using all of her strength, she climbed up to the lower bunk bed and then shimmied her way up to the top bunk. From there, it would be quite a leap over to the narrow window sill. Penny steadied herself, then ran along the length of the top bunk and jumped up towards the window.

She could not go very fast because of her injured leg, and when she made the leap she almost fell. But she managed to hang on, and she was able to slowly inch herself up and find her footing on the narrow stone ledge.

Penny looked out at the lights of the city across the harbor. She felt as her mother must have felt on her last night at Kingston. She had done her best with her life, and now her time was up.

****

Dinky was able to slowly navigate the streets of the city, and he finally found his old neighborhood. As he walked down the familiar street, he noticed for the first time all the carefully mowed lawns and the tidy gardens at each house. He was amazed at how different things looked from a human point of view. As a dog, he had paid no attention to any of it. When he reached his favorite fire hydrant, he stopped. How short it looked!

In his former dog-life, the fire hydrant had always seemed like a giant, red skyscraper.

A police cruiser stopped beside Dinky as he stood staring at the fire hydrant. The officer rolled down the window.

"Are you lost, sir?" the officer asked.

"No, just out for a walk," Dinky replied.

"Have a good evening, sir," the officer said.

A few steps more, and Dinky found himself in front of his house. The living room blinds were open, and he could see inside. His heart warmed at the sight of the pictures on the walls, the familiar furniture, all of the things he had once taken for granted. He was now home, and he would soon be part of the family again.

Dinky stood on the sidewalk and continued to look into the living room. He then saw Clyde Daniels enter the room, followed by Mary Daniels. They were smiling, and they looked excited. Then Daisy followed them into the living room, holding a little dog in her arms. Dinky watched as the family embraced their new pet. He lowered his eyes, and then continued on his way. He felt in that one instant that his whole life had been swept out from under him. He now had nothing.

Dinky made his way to a little park down the block. In his former life, Daisy had often taken him to this park while she played with her friends. The park was now deserted. Dinky went over to one of the swings and sat down. It was night, and the lights from the surrounding houses cast a faint glow all around him.

Then Dinky felt a chilly gust of wind and the sky seemed to darken. He then heard a familiar voice.

"Did you expect your family to grieve their loss forever?" the voice said.

Dinky looked around, and Miranda suddenly appeared on the swing next to him. The little angel-dog and angel-cat were playing happily at her feet.

"The lesson is a very simple one, Dinky," Miranda said. "They grieve their loss, and then they move on. Do you think this is your only lesson?"

Dinky only wanted to know one thing. "Will I see Penny again?" he asked.

Miranda smiled knowingly. "You have only one wish, and I told you to use it wisely."

There was desperation in Dinky's voice. "Then turn me back to what I was," he said.

"You wish to be an ugly dog again?"

"I will never wish for anything again, I swear!"

Miranda floated out of the swing and faced Dinky. She now had a grave expression, and there was an edge to her voice that made Dinky's heart start to pound.

"You were told that the one wish would not be easy," Miranda said. "And it appears you listened to some of the things you were told, but not others. Penny has been captured. She's been taken back to prison. And she is about to be marched down to that little room with the bright yellow door unless someone takes pity on her and saves her life."

Dinky was stunned. The angel-dog and the angel-cat now buzzed towards him to offer sympathy. There was a long silence.

"Maybe someone will adopt her," Dinky said, his voice choking. "A family, somewhere!"

"Perhaps," said Miranda.

Dinky sprang out of the swing and the little angel creatures went tumbling through the air.

"I don't believe you, anyway!" Dinky shouted.

"Oh, yes you do," Miranda said. "An unfortunate part of being human, is that deep down in their heart of hearts..."

Miranda now lowered her voice to a whisper.

"...people do believe bad news."

Dinky did not respond. He ran out of the park and bolted down the sidewalk.

****

The waves in Happy Valley harbor were choppy that night, and the summer storm blew a cold wind towards the shore. Dinky and Miranda stood alone on the shore and looked out at the prison. The gloomy stone building looked black against the night sky, except for a single light in one of the cell windows. This light was nothing more than a tiny square in the distance. But Dinky could see Penny's little silhouette outlined in the window. The image was as still as a painting on glass, and as black as the night itself.

"If you can grant wishes like you say you can, then you can do anything!" shouted Dinky, as the wind blew against him. "I want that ugly building blown to pieces!"

"Is that your wish?" Miranda asked. Her voice was calm, in contrast to the now-raging storm. "What about the same ugly building in the city next to us? Or the one after that? Why don't we journey round the world and save every dog and turn cats into dolphins and make the antelopes fly like eagles? Would that make the world a better place, do you think?"

Dinky did not respond.

"Dinky, do you understand now why all things must remain as God made them? More important, do you understand why it's God's plan that you remain exactly as He made you?"

Dinky gazed up at Penny's little shape in the window. In that same instant, the light went out and she was gone. He turned to Miranda.

"When you came to me that night," he said, "You said I could wish for anything if I didn't want to be a dog again."

"That's correct."

"You said you would put the wealth of the world at my feet."

"Yes, Dinky. You have one wish."

Dinky now spoke with all the conviction in his soul.

"Then I wish for Penny to find a home," he said quietly.

"And what about you, Dinky?"

Dinky looked at his outstretched hands. "I stay as you see me," he said.

"But what will become of you, Dinky?" Miranda asked. "The gift you give to Penny is the gift you once had and didn't want! It is something that will now be lost to you forever! You may not want to journey around the world with me and perform miracles, but you will wander the earth just the same! You will beg for every meal, and the echo of the thing you really are will haunt your every moment unto death!"

Miranda moved closer to Dinky. She still spoke quietly, but there was now steel beneath her words.

"She's just a stray dog. No one knows. No one cares. Wish for money, Dinky. Or power. I can give them to you!"

But Dinky knew exactly what he wanted. He had never been more certain about anything in his life.

"One thing is for sure," he smiled. "I don't have to worry about God's plan."

"Oh?" said Miranda, smiling back. "Why is that?"

"Because you made the promise to Penny's mother, and I will make it all come true!"

"Your wish is granted then!" said Miranda.

Miranda had no sooner spoken these few words when the storm passed and the moon came out from behind the clouds. The water was calm, and a warm breeze now drifted in from the harbor.

****

Penny was being marched towards the bright yellow door at the end of the cell block. She was carried by one of the prison guards. Behind her, the prison chaplain was muttering his words of comfort that no one could hear. Penny was taken slowly past the cells of all the other prisoners. They were all giving her a final farewell, just like they had done with Spike.

"Good-bye, little sister," said one dog.

"Chin up, girl!" said another. "Be strong, just like your mother."

"We're all in the same boat, Penny," said Nerd Dog. "They tell me I only got 24 hours."

A flash then went through Nerd Dog's mind. His eyes widened and he smiled brightly.

"Hey!" he shouted. "Is that 24 *dog hours*?"

The little procession stopped and everyone stared at Nerd Dog. Then Penny vanished.

"Where'd she go?" stammered the guard who had been holding her. "What happened?"

The other dogs now gave a rousing cheer.

Dinky and Miranda were still standing on the shore, and they could hear the faint echo of the cheering dogs. The sound soon faded away. Dinky gave Miranda a little smile, then he turned and started to walk down the long sidewalk that bordered the harbor road. Miranda let him go, but she called out to him before he passed out of sight.

"Oh, Dinky! You may be interested in knowing that I have never met Penny's mother! So I could not have made any promises to her! And if I did not make any promises, I don't have the foggiest notion who did. Do you? Or, do you think it's all a silly story?"

Dinky stopped in his tracks. He did not turn around.

"Can you do anything?" he shouted.

"Why do you ask?" Miranda shouted back.

"I have somewhere to go!" Dinky said.

"You know someone at this late hour, do you?" Miranda asked.

"I know where to look!" Dinky answered.

Miranda stood on the sidewalk and watched as Dinky continued along. He kept his back to her, and he did not tell her where he was going. But Miranda knew more about these things than Dinky could ever imagine.

****

Dinky walked through the deserted streets on the outskirts of the city. On one of the street corners he saw the homeless man with the dog on the leash and the shopping cart full of bottles and soda cans. The homeless man recognized Dinky and held up the familiar bottle.

"Hey!" said the man. "It's my old buddy! How about sharing a little gulp of the glad?"

Dinky stopped and took the bottle. He swirled the contents around, then raised the bottle to his lips. "I've never tried after shave before," Dinky said, just before drinking. "First time for everything!"

"It's Windex," the dog said.

Dinky paused, then handed the bottle back and continued on his way.

****

The old Feed and Tack warehouse on Water street lay deserted. The dogs had all gone, and the building was silent. Dinky saw that the front door had now been locked with a single padlock after the police raid a few nights ago. The wood frame around the door was splintered and rotting, and with a little effort Dinky had no problem forcing the door open.

Dinky stepped inside the cavernous building and made his way across the broken glass and debris and all the cobwebs to the stairway on the far side. Cautiously, he began to climb up the stairs to the rooftop. The stairs groaned under his weight, and each step he took raised a tiny cloud of dust under his feet.

Dinky reached the top step and tried the door. It had not been locked, and it creaked open. He stepped out onto the rooftop.

The sky was perfectly clear, and the whole city was shining under the light of the full moon.

Dinky looked around. He saw nothing, and all he could hear was the peck-peck-peck sound of some nearby pigeons. A few seconds passed, then Dinky heard something down at his feet. It was a squeaking sound. He looked down, and saw a tiny newborn puppy nuzzling his shoe. He reached down and scooped the little creature up in the palm of his hand and held it close to his cheek.

"Hey, little fella," Dinky whispered. "Where's your momma?"

Dinky heard the same squeaking sound again, and noticed that a few more newborn puppies had gathered around his feet. They circled around him, then began to walk one by one towards the back of the shelter that protected the rooftop door. Dinky watched them go, then he followed behind.

When he reached the other side of the shelter, he saw the mother dog. Her nine healthy puppies surrounded her. The mother dog lay on her side, exhausted. Her eyes were closed and she was breathing heavily. She was cradling her last puppy close to her body. This newborn was the runt of the litter, a sickly looking dog that did not look like it could possibly make it through the night. The little dog was all black like her nine brothers, but she had a tiny patch of white fur on her forehead in the shape of a diamond.

Dinky knelt down and stroked the head of the mother dog.

She could barely move. She still had her eyes closed, and she gently licked Dinky's hand. Dinky then gave the sickly looking newborn dog a very light stroke on the top of her head with the back of his finger. The tiny dog made a very faint squealing sound and nuzzled up closer to her mother. The other puppies stayed close, but they did not interfere.

Dinky again stroked the mother dog's head and this time she managed to wag her tail ever so slightly. Her eyes were still closed, and her chest was slowly rising and falling with each heavy, measured breath she took.

"I knew I'd find you here," Dinky whispered. "Now that doesn't make a lotta sense, does it? But I knew it just the same."

Dinky leaned closer and whispered into the mother dog's ear.

"I'm here to bring you some very good news tonight," he said. "Life isn't going to be an easy one for you. But you know that already, don't you? I'm here to tell you that this little one, the one that almost killed you to bring into this world – she'll be fine. She will live, and she will be taken into the home of a family who will love her. And that is my promise to you."

The mother dog summoned all her effort and opened her sad, tired eyes.

"Just hold your daughter close," Dinky said. "And sleep. We're both going to sleep."

The mother dog slowly closed her eyes and slept. Dinky gave her head a final stroke.

It was God's plan that he should make this promise, and his journey was now over.

Dinky walked over to the edge of the roof and looked down.

He paused, then stepped up onto the ledge. He swayed a little, then caught his balance. He looked out at all the lights of the city, and he was reminded of a thought he had earlier that day when he was watching the people in the town square. Everyone out there had a purpose and a destination.

Dinky looked up at the full moon, the eternal frozen face. He imagined himself as he might look from the ground, a matchstick man against the night sky, bathed in moonlight. Dinky closed his eyes and held out his arms. Voices from his past now echoed around him.

"Here Daisy! We bought you a little dog," said Clyde.

"I love him Daddy. I'll name him Dinky!" said Daisy.

"Where's that ugly little dog?" said Esther.

"I'm askin' you what Penny's mother asked me the night she took the Big Ride at Kingston. Take care of her," said Spike.

"Remember the wish. The thing you so desperately want will not be as you think. And the one wish will not be easy," said Miranda.

Then Dinky heard the sound of his own voice.

"If you can grant wishes like you say you can, then you can do anything!"

The voices then melted together into the sounds of laughter. There was the laughter from the crowd at the fair, and laughter from the guests at the party. Dinky teetered a bit on the rooftop ledge.

Then, he leaned forward and jumped.

Immediately, the laughter stopped and he could hear the sound of his own voice once again.

"Anything! Anything!"

Dinky was now a dog again, spinning through the air. He landed with a thump on his doggie-bed in Daisy's room, took a high bounce, and ended up flat on his back on the floor. It took a few moments for him to compose himself. He could hear the sounds of the party downstairs.

Dinky looked up and found that he had landed directly beneath the doggie-clock on the wall.

The time was exactly 9:30.

Chapter 10
(Happy At Last)

The party was fast becoming a social triumph for Mary Daniels. Mary was especially thrilled that Mayor Briggs and his wife Esther were having such a splendid time. The ugly family dog was the star of the show, and everyone wanted Daisy to go upstairs and bring the dog down for some picture taking.

"I've waited long enough, child," laughed Esther Briggs, holding up her camera. "You just run upstairs and fetch that little doggie! I simply have to have a picture, or no one on this earth will believe me!"

Daisy smiled and ran upstairs to fetch Dinky. When she reached her bedroom, she flung the door open.

"Dinky!" Daisy shouted, brimming with excitement. "Oh, Dinky! You are the most famous dog in all of Happy Valley!"

Before Daisy could take another step, Miranda's image appeared directly in front of her. Daisy did not see anything, and she simply passed through the brightly colored image as she charged into the bedroom. But as soon as she had done this, Daisy's expression changed. She stopped and looked around. Her dolls were carefully lined up on her bed like they always were, the furniture was just the same, and even the tick-tick-ticking of the doggie-clock was the same sound she had always known. Yet the room was somehow different. All her life she had looked at everything in that room through the same bratty-kid eyes, but a different person now looked down upon the timid creature in the doggie-bed. It was time for Daisy Daniels to grow up.

Dinky watched as Daisy approached. He was frightened, and he trembled when she touched him. Daisy carefully picked him up and gently rocked the quivering little bundle in her arms.

"Dinky, you've been crying!" Daisy said, in a voice Dinky had never heard from her before.

Daisy placed him back in the little bed. She took off the pink bonnet and the frilly pink shorts, crumpling the outfit into a ball and tossing it across the room.

"From now on, no more stupid outfits," she said. "And no more contests, either. I'm sorry, Dinky."

In the kitchen, the parakeet and the goldfish had been motionless and staring. They now relaxed, and all was back to normal.

In the living room, the party guests had all assembled at the foot of the stairs waiting for Daisy to come back down with the World's Ugliest Mutt in her arms. But when she came out of her bedroom she was alone.

"Where's that dog, child?" Esther Briggs demanded. "My trigger finger is getting cramps!"

Daisy said nothing. She walked down the staircase and went up to her father. The buzzing of the party guests died down and everyone stared at her.

"I don't want people laughing at Dinky any more," Daisy said.

Daisy then went over to her mother, who could not understand the sudden change in her daughter's behavior.

"And we won't be dressing him up, either," she said to Mary.

"Yes, of course," Mary said, looking uneasily around the room.

Daisy then turned her attention to Esther Briggs.

"If you think a person looks funny, do you walk up to them and laugh and take a picture?"

"Well!" she exclaimed. Esther looked over at her husband. "Harold, the Van Dusens have invited us over, and if we're going to go and not put anyone's nose out of joint, then we better drink up!"

"I suppose," said Mayor Briggs.

The front doorbell rang. Clyde quickly moved across the room and opened the door.

Two dog pound officials stood at the door. They both wore crisp, new uniforms. They had a small dog cage placed between them on the porch. One of the pound officials had a name tag that read 'Mr. Pettkus'. The other had a name tag that read 'Mr. Levitts'. Behind them stood their faithful canine companion Rex, happily wagging his tail.

"Is this the Daniels residence?" asked Mr. Pettkus politely.

"Yes," Clyde responded. "Come in!"

The two men picked up the cage and carried it into the hall. Rex followed behind.

"Beautiful home you have here, sir!" Mr. Pettkus exclaimed, looking around. "The front lawn, each blade of grass looks manicured. I try to achieve that look with my own lawn, but it is quite a challenge when your lawn is green cement!"

As Mr. Pettkus laughed at his own joke, Mr. Levitts turned his attention to Mary Daniels.

"Are you the lady of the house?" he asked.

Mary ignored him. "Clyde, what is this?" she demanded. "Who are these men?"

"I just love your colors, ma'am," said Mr. Levitts.

"Thank you!" Mary snapped. "Clyde!"

"So warm and inviting," said Mr. Levitts. "I keep telling the Mrs. that I would love some new color around our house, but unfortunately she takes it personally and then strikes me with her fist!"

The guests all gathered around as Mr. Levitts opened the animal cage and took out a tiny little dog. This dog was all black, but had a white patch of fur on her forehead in the distinctive shape of a diamond. Mary was astonished.

"What on earth..." she said. "Clyde, what is this? Another pet in the house?"

"Her name is Penny," said Mr. Levitts. "We try to discourage the use of the term 'pet' around our animals, ma'am. I appreciate you have the best of motives, but it is so impersonal."

Clyde took Penny from Mr. Levitts and carefully handed her over to Daisy. Daisy was thrilled.

"Clyde, we can't have another pet!" Mary insisted.

"Now this is the strangest thing..." Clyde began.

The guests now gathered closer to Clyde and listened.

"I was in town the other day at the pet store buying Dinky's food. I'm in the store when all of a sudden, well, you're going to think this is a little crazy, but all of a sudden all the animals in the place were frozen, and staring. The birds, the fish, the hamsters in their cages, all of them! They were all staring out the window towards that awful dog prison way out in the harbor!"

"Why sir!" interrupted Mr. Levitts, "The architecture may be lacking..."

"But we assure you the dogs are treated like royalty," added Mr. Pettkus.

"And every dog finds a home!" said Mr. Levitts.

"And we keep them happy and healthy until they do!" screamed Mr. Pettkus.

The guests stared at Mr. Pettkus. He gave an embarrassed half-smile and took a step back.

"Well," said Clyde, "I just had to take the little boat ride over and have a look around. The very first dog I saw was little Penny here, and I thought – heck, she'll make a perfect companion for Dinky."

"She *is* perfect, Daddy," said Daisy. "Thank you!"

"Just a minute here," Mary said, stepping forward. "I was not consulted about this, and I do not want another dog in this house!"

There was silence now as the party guests all turned their attention to Clyde.

Mary was insistent. "I don't want to be a spoiler here," she said, "But that dog will just have to be taken back!"

Clyde looked around at all the people now staring at him. He took a deep breath and turned to Mary.

"My dear Mary," he began, "We've been married for fifteen years and I wouldn't trade a day of those fifteen years for anything else in the world. You've been a good mother, and a good wife, and you keep a wonderful home. Our company here has you alone to thank for arranging this wonderful party. I certainly had nothing to do with it – other than footing the bill for all the food and liquor!"

The guests all laughed, then quickly fell silent again.

"I intend to keep a manicured lawn exactly the way you insist a manicured lawn should look," Clyde continued. "And every Spring I will spread a generous helping of steer manure on that manicured lawn, and I'll even hold my nose and do it twice if that's what it takes to make you happy."

Mary had never heard this tone from her husband, and her first instinct was to run from the room. Her legs wouldn't move.

"But, we *are* having another dog in the house," Clyde said, pointing to Penny. "*That* dog. And if you wish to discuss this now, then I will be forced to raise my voice in front of our guests. Shall I raise my voice?"

Mary stared at Clyde. She was speechless. None of the guests said a word. Then, Esther Briggs stepped forward and took Mary by the arm.

"Mary Daniels," she said, "I've been thinking. We need a new chairperson for the Heritage Committee and you'd be absolutely perfect for the job!"

Esther then led Mary into the kitchen. "And while we're at it," Esther said, "I would love another cup of tea. And this one can have a good shot of brandy in it! Lovely party my dear! The best I have ever attended!"

All attention was now turned to Daisy and Penny. Everyone crowded around them and gently patted Penny's head. One of the guests then saw Dinky standing at the top of the stairs.

"Hey! There he is!"

Everyone stared up at Dinky. Dinky stared back. Daisy then placed Penny on the bottom step and the guests all watched as the little dog climbed the stairs. Dinky didn't dare to even blink. When Penny reached the top step, she gave Dinky a good sniffing. Dinky continued to remain motionless. Once Penny was done with her inspection, the two dogs trotted side by side down the hallway towards Daisy's bedroom. They slipped through the narrow crack in the door, and the guests all laughed as Dinky gently shut the door with his paw. Everyone broke into wild applause.

The party was the talk of the town for months. At long last, Mary Daniels had found her place at the pinnacle of Happy Valley Society - ugly dogs and all.

****

Clyde saw Mr. Pettkus and Mr. Levitts to the door. Rex was with them, still wagging his tail.

"Do I owe you fellows anything?" Clyde said. "I forgot to ask."

"Oh, no sir," said Mr. Pettkus. "We work for a charitable organization."

"However," added Mr. Levitts, "It's a well-known fact that no charity ever turns down a donation!"

"Point taken," said Clyde. "Thank you, gentlemen!"

"Come on, Rex!" shouted Mr. Pettkus.

The two dog pound officials walked down the front steps and headed towards their vehicle. Rex followed happily behind. When they reached the sidewalk, Mr. Pettkus stopped and looked back towards the house. Clyde waved to them, and then closed the front door. Mr. Pettkus seemed to be preoccupied with something.

"What is it?" Mr. Levitts asked him.

"That other dog, the ugly one," said Mr. Pettkus. "I've seen it somewhere before."

"How long have you been working for the canine society?" asked Mr. Levitts.

"Over forty years," came the reply.

"You see most everything in forty years," said Mr. Levitts.

They all piled into the van and drove away. As they headed down the street, Rex had the sense that there was something on the street behind them. Mr. Pettkus and Mr. Levitts were chatting away in the front seat, and they did not notice anything. But Rex knew they were being followed. He put his nose up to the side window and barked.

"You want some fresh air, boy?" said Mr. Pettkus. "That what you want?"

Mr. Pettkus then pressed a button and lowered the window. Rex stuck his head out and looked back down the street. His instincts had been correct.

Running after them were two stray dogs. One of the dogs wore thick eye glasses with tape in the middle of the black frames. The other dog was wearing a gold name tag with the words spelled out in Latin. This dog would have been a tough-looking dog in any group – except that he, too, wore thick eye glasses with tape. In fact, the lenses in his glasses were even thicker, and the huge black frames had even more tape! Two homeless nerds, thought Rex. Poor fellows!

Rex pulled his head back into the van and barked happily. The dogs still ran after the van.

"Remember us, Rex?" shouted Nerd Dog.

"Can we hang with you, Rex?" shouted Nerd Spike.

"*Don't leave us Rex!*" they both shouted in unison.

Everyone knows that dogs don't talk, but someone in Happy Valley must have heard the shouts of Nerd Dog and Nerd Spike as they followed the van all the way back into town.

****

My name is Dinky, and I am one ugly dog! Heck, I'd look better if they shaved my butt and walked me backwards! But, I am Dinky the dog and on this earth there is no one else like me. I have learned my lesson, and I am so grateful at last for that half-acre of happiness that I now call home.

My little tale is over now. But before I go, I want you to give a thought to all the ugly dogs out there in the cold, cruel world.

People, we know we're ugly! So be kind to us! And please, please, try not to laugh. Dinky the dog is here to tell you that there are angels among us, and those angels can teach a lesson to just about anybody! So if one day you find yourself at an ugly mutt contest, take a good look around you before the curtains go up and the crowd starts laughing. If the angels have their way, we ugly dogs may be the ones sitting in the crowd. And when the first trembling creature hits the floodlights – the crowd may be laughing at you!

THE END

Made in the USA
Charleston, SC
06 February 2012